NO WILLPOWER
REQUIRED

D1528232

NO WILLPOWER REQUIRED

A neuroscience approach to change your habits with alcohol

Copyright © 2024 Michael Hardenbrook.

All rights reserved. No part of this publication may be used or reproduced in any manner whatsoever without written permission except in the case of short excerpts used in published reviews.

Printed in the United States of America

NO WILLPOWER
REQUIRED

A neuroscience approach to change
your habits with alcohol

MICHAEL HARDENBROOK

CONTENTS

The author of this book does not give medical advice or prescribe any technique or drug as a treatment for medical, physical, or mental problems. The author intends to share information of a general nature based on his personal journey to wellness. If you choose to use any information in this book for yourself, the author and the publisher assume no responsibility for your actions.

R.E.S.E.T Guidebook

Before embarking on the transformative journey this book promises, there's something you should do first. To ensure you get the most out of each chapter, I've designed a 66-Day R.E.S.E.T. Guidebook. This is your roadmap through every step, every concept, and every action point of the book.

As more research and insights emerge, I regularly add new resources to make sure you're always equipped with the latest knowledge.

Before you turn the page to the first chapter, take a moment to head over to hardenbrook.com/nwr or scan the QR code for the guidebook and access all the additional resources to help support your success.

I dedicate this book to Priscilla, my guiding North Star, and to Hailey, Ethan, Andrew, and Carter, the constellations that brighten my world. Through your light, I see clearly, and within your love, I find endless inspiration.

PART

01

Alcohol Effect

"The strength of our future isn't in the might of our dreams, but in the diligence of our daily habits."

- MIKE HARDENBROOK

New Perspective

Forget what you think you know about quitting alcohol—this is a reinvention, not a restriction. Whether you're here to simply understand your drinking habits or to embark on a transformative change, give yourself a pat on the back. It's courageous even to consider examining the shadows cast by something so celebrated in our culture. If you're not ready to get started today, that's okay. As you progress through this book, you'll discover your unique starting point, free from pressure and full of promise.

This isn't your typical guide that might preach permanent abstinence, stamp you with a label, or dangle the carrot of financial savings. Instead, it's about aligning your relationship with alcohol to your broader life goals—much like maintaining a balanced diet, keeping fit, or excelling in your career.

In this comprehensive guide, we will unveil the mysteries behind the power of choice and control. We'll examine the intricacies of alcohol consumption, from habits to the revelations of neuroscience. This is your toolbox, meticulously curated with powerful strategies that have transformed countless lives.

We will explore various aspects of alcohol consumption, including habits, personal growth, and neuroscience. You'll gain the knowledge and tools to transform your life using proven methods from motivational enhancement therapy (MET), cognitive-behavioral therapy (CBT), habit reversal training (HRT), and neuroscience research.

These approaches are effective in helping people achieve their goals. I've woven them into the fabric of this book without explicitly labeling them. The inclusion of neuroscience further supports the efficacy of these techniques by providing a deeper understanding of the brain's role in behavioral change.

Motivational enhancement therapy (MET) helps you examine your motivations, clarify your reasons for change, and set well-defined goals. It lays the groundwork for moving forward with practical steps and renewed commitment. Since its introduction in 1992, MET has had an estimated 80% success rate.

Cognitive-behavioral therapy (CBT) has a success rate between 50% and 75%. CBT helps alleviate anxiety, depression, and alcohol use by teaching you to recognize connections between thoughts, feelings, and actions. We'll explore these connections to understand how they influence your drinking.

Habit reversal training (HRT) is a behavioral therapy that helps you identify and permanently change unwanted habits. Various HRT studies have shown promising results, with success rates ranging from 60% to 80% in reducing alcohol consumption.

Neuroscience provides valuable insights into the brain's role in habit formation and the underlying mechanisms associated with alcohol consumption. Understanding the neural pathways involved in alcohol-related behaviors and how they are rewired through therapeutic techniques will help us address your alcohol-related challenges and create lasting change.

By integrating these diverse approaches, this guide offers a comprehensive, evidence-based roadmap for transforming your life and achieving your goals around alcohol. Let's review a breakdown of what we will cover in each section of the book:

Part 1: Alcohol's Impact on Our Lives
Uncover the effects of alcohol, offering a fresh perspective and highlighting the often-overlooked "in-between drinkers." We discuss the 70/20/10 statistics of alcohol consumption, its influence on brain chemistry, and reasons some people opt for moderation or total abstention.

Part 2: Understanding Habits & The Wonders of Neuroscience
Journey into the science of habits and the intricate world of neuroscience. Gain insights into brain mechanisms that drive habit formation and change. By grasping concepts like synaptic plasticity, neurogenesis, and neuroplasticity, you'll be better positioned to navigate your relationship with alcohol.

Part 3: External Influences & Personal Choices
Explore the external forces shaping our alcohol habits. Equip yourself to handle social situations involving alcohol, manage stress, reclaim lost time, and utilize powerful tools such as manifestation and journaling to aid your transformation journey.

Part 4: Tools & Techniques for Transformation
Discover a range of strategies to reshape your habits. From initiating your transformation journey to handling setbacks, we'll introduce tools like urge surfing, meditation, and breathwork to strengthen your control and emotional balance.

Part 5: Prioritizing Well-being – Mind & Body
Provides strategies to support your mental and physical well-being. Collaborating with a doctor specializing in addiction relief, we have crafted an in-depth suggested supplement guide to support your body as you navigate this change. We recommend you work with your doctor to determine if these suggestions align with your current health situation. Additionally, understand the vital roles of sleep, exercise, meditation, and breathwork in supporting your holistic well-being. By nurturing your mind and body, you'll be better prepared to face the challenges and reap the rewards of your journey.

Part 6: Exploring Alternative Approaches

Presents alternative approaches to support your transformation, exploring the potential benefits of options like cannabis, psychedelics, EMDR therapy, TMS treatment, and virtual reality. Considering these alternatives, you can make informed decisions about what might work best for your situation.

Finally, we will guide you through planning for your future, with strategies for self-evaluation, adjusting to life after transformation, and addressing the challenges that may arise as you maintain your new relationship with alcohol. You'll be encouraged to reflect on your experiences, growth, and goals throughout the process.

This isn't just a book. It's your playbook. You're unlocking a powerhouse of inner strength using the tried-and-true methods of MET, CBT, and HRT. Are you ready to take the first step? Let's begin this transformation together.

Self-Assessment

"I am not what happened to me, I am what I choose to become."

– CARL JUNG

Many programs or books begin with a questionnaire, a self-assessment designed to categorize your current drinking with a label. I consciously decided to omit that typical path. The fact that you are reading this suggests that you have already decided to seek change. From my perspective, does it truly matter to define that decision within the confines of a label?

Let's review my personal experience with the term "alcoholic." In my youth, drinking was part of the experience. College times were filled with excitement; studying all week, and then Friday afternoons marked the start of the party. I would usually head to a friend's apartment in the same complex for some pre-gaming. It was the typical college scene with a group of guys, cases of Keystone Light, banter, and laughter, all getting ready for a night out. Those nights were always unpredictable, with lots of drinking, rowdiness, and the inevitable morning-after hangover. Looking back, I do not regret those days. I was experimenting, being free in my youth. However, as I transitioned into adulthood, drinking took on a different place in my life. It was no longer the carefree, exciting experience that I once enjoyed; it became a coping mechanism after a tough day or a challenge to decline in social situations, even when I intended to abstain.

I found it increasingly difficult to adopt a take-it-or-leave-it attitude, so I began to question, "Am I an alcoholic?" This marked a shift in my mindset. Rather than unconsciously continuing my drinking, I started to explore the nature of my relationship with alcohol. The term "alcoholic" was the first that came to mind when addressing an unhealthy relationship with alcohol.

I remember typing into Google "How do I know if I'm an alcoholic?" I took several self-assessment questionnaires, but the results didn't reveal anything I wasn't already aware of regarding my drinking. I knew I drank more than I wanted to at times. It was possible my drinking had reached a level where it could be labeled. For some reason, I felt compelled to compare my drinking to others, searching for answers to my issue. It's curious when you think about it. When we experience depression, we don't seek a label for that depression; we seek a solution. We don't compare the intensity of our depression with others. Similarly, when we struggle with anxiety, we don't need confirmation of our anxiety; we seek remedies. The level of anxiety defined by others doesn't affect our determination to change. That's precisely how I felt during those moments. I didn't need someone to label my problem; I was very aware of it. I didn't fixate on the level or definition of the problem; it was a problem for me. My focus was on finding a solution, and I didn't believe that labeling it would improve or expedite the problem-solving process.

Fast forward to the present; reflecting on this journey. It's common for us to attempt to categorize and label things, believing it's the first step towards addressing them. While this approach is effective in many cases, I've come to see labeling as a narrow perspective. It restricts our understanding of the issue, confining it to the boundaries of traditional solutions. I've often wondered why we feel compelled to assign labels. The concept of labeling holds significant importance in the 12-step community, where the first step to recovery is publicly admitting that you're an alcoholic. However, this labeling never resonated with me; not because I lacked the motivation to change, but because something about that path didn't align with what I needed for real transformation. Something about the label felt unnecessary.

I didn't connect with a solution that required me to declare that I was an alcoholic and utterly powerless over alcohol. Deep down, I knew that I possessed the power to change, and a label wouldn't ignite that desire.

I gradually realized that the journey toward change wasn't about adopting a label; it was about comprehending my motivations, identifying my triggers, and recognizing my capacity for change. It was about taking back control of my life from the grips of alcohol, not through a label, but through a deliberate, conscious choice to transform.

So, here's where I'm going with all of this. My experience is unique to me, and I encountered a disconnect with the idea of labeling. There's nothing wrong with assigning a label if it leads to positive change. However, the way we label ourselves can influence our self-perception and decision-making. For some, labeling is empowering, but for others, it has the opposite effect. For those of us in the latter group, adopting a label like "alcoholic" can fundamentally alter how we view ourselves and our potential for change. Labels can lock us into a fixed mindset, where we begin to define ourselves solely through the lens of that label, often overlooking other aspects of our identity. This can create a self-fulfilling prophecy, where our behavior aligns more closely with the label over time. Moreover, decision-making can often be swayed by labels, influenced more by the expected limitations or implications of the label, rather than by our own objectives. I believe that comprehending this impact is vital in addressing and reshaping one's relationship with alcohol, as it opens the door to a more comprehensive and empowering self-perspective.

The reason I chose to explore labeling is the connection to the idea of a solution. Labels are closely tied to 12-step programs, which have been life-changing and life-saving solutions for many. Are they the perfect solution? They are—for those they work for. If you decide to commit to Sober October with a group of friends and find yourself extending it to two months, then three, gradually drinking only occasionally or not at all, that's a perfect solution. If you can pull off sheer determination and willpower to stop drinking, that's a perfect solution. If you can pick up a book and discover a path that aligns with your goals, that's a perfect solution. As you can probably guess, the perfect solution is whatever works best for you, without the need for a label. What proves effective for one person may not be suitable for another, and that's perfectly perfect. What worked for one might not work for another, and that is okay.

The journey toward change is unique, and the solution that works for you is a personal discovery. It's not about adhering to a universally accepted method, but about finding a combination of strategies and insights that resonate with your individual experiences and goals.

This realization was liberating. It meant that my path to change didn't have to fit a conventional mold; it could be as unique as my own experiences. This is what I'd like to pass on to you as we move forward. This is your journey to create the path that feels authentic to you. That is the perfect solution for your goals.

Overview:

- The insignificance of self-assessment questionnaires and the use of labels.
- A shift in mindset from unconscious drinking to self-exploration, including the consideration of whether the label "alcoholic" applies.
- Labeling can confine individuals to fixed mindsets and influence decision-making, leading to the belief that understanding this impact is crucial in reshaping one's relationship with alcohol.
- Embrace a non-conventional path to change; the journey towards personal growth doesn't require adhering to universally accepted methods or labels.

In-between Drinkers

"The trouble with labels is that they are limiting. They lead to stereotypes, expectations, and judgments that can be difficult to shake off."

- PHILIP HENSHER.

Traditionally, there have been two labels around alcohol in society. The spectrum ranges from those who abstain or have a healthy relationship with alcohol to those with severe alcohol use disorders (AUD). AUD is the medical term where a person's alcohol consumption harms their life, health, and relationships. Common characteristics of AUD include:

- An inability to control or reduce alcohol intake.
- An intense craving for alcohol.
- Continued use despite harmful consequences.

On the other side of the coin, there is everyone else. Everyone else falls into the category of "healthy drinkers." This category is essential for understanding and addressing one's relationship with alcohol. However, "healthy" is such an open-ended label, there is a middle ground that often goes unmentioned. This binary labeling leaves most people under-served, without guidance for changing their habits. "In-between drinkers" offers a broader perspective that recognizes the complexity of human behaviors and experiences with alcohol. It reflects a spectrum of drinking, highlighting the fluidity and changeability of our relationship with alcohol.

In-between drinking refers to alcohol consumption patterns between moderate and healthy drinking. This term is descriptive, not prescriptive, and it does not dictate a person's identity or future behavior. Unlike labels like "alcoholic," which can carry a sense of permanence and inevitability, "in-between drinkers" allows for growth and change. The main difference between in-between drinkers (often referred to as gray area drinkers) and those with alcohol use disorder (AUD) is their level of control over their drinking habits and how much it impacts their lives. While they might occasionally overdo it, in-between drinkers usually don't experience severe consequences or a complete loss of control. These drinkers may not exhibit the signs of addiction or dependence in those with severe alcohol use disorders. However, they may still experience some negative consequences due to their alcohol consumption.

According to the CDC, one in three adults who drink can be classified as excessive drinkers, and the majority of them indulge in binge drinking on multiple occasions. However, nine out of ten excessive drinkers are not alcohol dependent (89.8%: excessive drinkers who are not dependent, 10.2%: excessive drinkers who are dependent).

For non-alcohol dependent individuals, why is it so hard to take a break? Those labeled alcoholics often experience a defining moment that prompts a need for significant changes. This moment varies greatly and can include losing everything; a job, family, or home. For others, it might be a medical scare. For these individuals, continuing to drink becomes unbearable, forcing them to stop, and is often a life-or-death decision.

On the other hand, you and I might consider limiting or quitting alcohol to elevate our lives— improving our health, reducing anxiety, enhancing clarity, or achieving better sleep. As with weight-loss (where some people face serious health risks, while others aim to shed those last ten pounds), the experience of in-between drinkers is not fixed and can evolve over time. There's always a reason to break our commitment to change; vacations, holiday dinners, happy hours, and more.

Identifying In-Between Drinkers: To determine whether you might be in this category, consider the following signs and characteristics:

Inconsistency: Your drinking patterns may vary, sometimes moderate or occasional, and other times more excessive.

Ambivalence: You have mixed feelings about your alcohol consumption, enjoying the social aspects while recognizing its potential negative consequences.

Functioning: Despite your alcohol consumption, you maintain your personal and professional responsibilities, making it more challenging for you to recognize any negative issues.

Control: You may be able to control your drinking in certain situations or for specific periods but struggle with self-control in others.

Absence of Severe Consequences: If you have not experienced severe effects from alcohol use, such as significant health issues, legal troubles, or damaged relationships, you still may experience some negative impacts, like occasional hangovers or feelings of guilt and shame.

By moving beyond traditional labels, we also move away from the stigma that they carry. A stigma that can influence how we define ourselves. Describing someone as an in-between drinker recognizes their unique position and experiences without the negative connotations associated with labels like alcoholic. This allows us, as individuals, to focus on our unique paths towards a healthier relationship with alcohol, free from the constraints of societal labeling.

Within in-between drinking, we have a lot of variation, which makes it hard to define. You have some who struggle to break free from the nightly ritual of wine. In contrast, there may be others who can abstain all week but spend weekends overindulging. Others may have a few drinks here and there, where it slowly builds up in quantity over time until they decide to quit for a while. These are three very distinct types of relationships with alcohol that could have their own labels. We are all unique, with some overlap in experience. We each will have our unique drinking scenario.

Let me lay out three fictional characters and backgrounds related to these labels for these three scenarios. Read them and see if you can identify with some of their experience.

Chris is 42 and began drinking at parties in high school and college. Chris never felt like he fit in. Drinking made him feel good in social settings. In his twenties, he overindulged at social gatherings but still met his work obligations. As time went on, he socialized less and less. Having a few drinks made him feel like the same fun-loving guy. Chris routinely picked up a bottle of wine at the store. He didn't keep alcohol in the house or drink hard liquor but did enjoy an evening of kicking back. He usually finished most of it and could wake up the next day ready to get on with his day. Chris continued this habit for several years without considering it a problem. However, his tolerance increased over time, and one bottle became closer to two.

Additionally, with age, Chris began to feel hungover in the mornings. He spent his day barely managing to feel better. He would miss work on some days. His alcohol habit began to cause him anxiety and trouble falling asleep well. But he believed that if he didn't have a bottle of wine, he wouldn't be able to fall asleep. His drinking habit had become a problem. Chris looked into some options on Google, but all he found were in-patient or AA programs to deal with his drinking. Chris wasn't sure if he wanted to stop completely, but he knew his relationship with alcohol was unhealthy, and he needed to make a change.

Christina grew up in a conservative family. She didn't drink in high school. She would drink occasionally in college but never to excess. As an adult, she sometimes drank at a party but didn't give drinking much thought outside those settings. Then after having three kids, she began to buy wine to drink in the evening to wind down –at first, never a lot. However, having a few drinks turned into drinking an entire bottle. The alcohol didn't affect her day-to-day. She didn't feel hungover or bad. But she began to think that having wine was becoming a habit. She has been struggling to lose weight and knows too well that regular drinking is getting in the way. She also tends to snack more when she drinks, adding to her weight problem. So, in the morning, she says, "Tonight I won't have that wine." But after a long day of work and coming home to care for her kids, she waffles and convinces herself that a glass or two can't hurt. So, she decides tomorrow will be a better day to stop, and this decision becomes a repeating pattern. The motivation or pain to stop isn't strong enough. Christina never sought ways to prevent or consider the need for a program. However, she wants to break the habit of reaching her physical and health goals and needs a reliable plan to get her there. Even though she doesn't have what you would call a problematic drinking situation, she still finds it difficult to stop.

Wayne is 34 and has worked since he was out of high school. He did well in high school, played football, and was on the wrestling team. After graduation, he worked in sales. His job required him to travel. While on the road, he would have a few drinks at happy hour. He sometimes would have too many at a few events and said things while drinking he regretted later. However, come Monday, Wayne was back at work without a drop. Wayne is a big football fan, and he meets with friends on the weekend to watch games. Watching football and drinking beer is what men are supposed to do. Like the sales events, Wayne started to overindulge. Why not? He's worked hard all week. Most of the time, Wayne drinks without incident. However, at times it causes him to do things he never would do.

One Sunday morning, Wayne wakes up and remembers getting into an out-of-control yelling match the night before with one of his friends. In this state, Wayne then drove home. He swears off drinking forever. However, a week goes by, the pain has subsided, and the chance to get together with his drinking buddies is calling his name. He goes, of course, and his friends have pitchers of beer waiting for him on the table. Wayne is struggling to have the willpower not to drink. He is also troubled by the need to explain to his friends why he's not drinking. Under this peer pressure, he gives in and repeats his drinking pattern. As a high-achieving sales guy, Wayne is tired of spending his weekends drinking and being unproductive. The weekends don't feel like weekends, and he is tired and worn out on Mondays.

Wayne regrets that he was unable to break the habit with willpower alone. He feels weak and stuck. Wayne thinks about what he could be doing on his goals list –hiking the local mountain or learning Spanish for his upcoming trip to Costa Rica. Wayne wants to change his relationship with alcohol but doesn't know how to break free of the cycle.

You can see that these three examples depict a very different relationship with alcohol with one common factor: a desire to change the relationship with alcohol but no clear path on how to do that.

Any leader of a sobriety program will tell you that if you are questioning your relationship with alcohol, you are an alcoholic. In my view, this labeling is incorrect for almost everyone. It is necessary for some. Societal norms suggest that if we aren't full-blown alcoholics beside a dumpster or with a hard life, our relationship with alcohol is normal. It is my contention to argue that there is a group that falls between alcoholics and take-it-or-leave-it drinkers. This in-between group has had enough alcohol to start questioning their relationship with alcohol and needs support to change their habit.

Unlike those with alcohol use disorder, in-between-drinkers may not experience a "rock bottom" moment that compels them to stop drinking. Initiating a meaningful shift in drinking habits without support is challenging. Societal norms and aggressive marketing convey a message that alcohol is necessary to have a good time. The bar is the center of every good party. Sitting on the beach isn't as good unless we have a Corona or frozen drink beside the beach chair. For whatever reason, you seek a way to improve yourself by changing your relationship with alcohol. You may find it challenging to reduce or quit drinking alcohol. Until now, the only options were AA or some 12-step program.

I define in-between drinkers as a group motivated to change but having difficulty understanding how to make that change. I'm not going to sugarcoat it. Making the change may be less straightforward than it is for others with deeper issues with alcohol. For alcoholics, the answer is easy: stop or die. However, in-between drinkers have no clear definition or path. Aside from the obvious, I use the term in-between to demonstrate that you are in between two labels as we traditionally define them. Normal and alcoholic. And being in between, you could move from one end to the other of both labels through intention and behavior. It's possible to let bad lifestyle choices move you closer to the alcoholic level. Most alcoholics don't immediately become that way. They did so over time, wrapped up in a vicious cycle without even realizing it. The same goes for light and infrequent drinkers. It's also possible over time to shift from in-between to a light-drinker with the right amount of cessation coupled with a mental reframing around what place alcohol has in your life. You can go from the farthest end of the pendulum and completely give up alcohol. At that point, it's lost all value in your life. It's a choice that becomes evident. It's not a sacrifice but a choice. When you reframe your thinking, you make a choice, not a sacrifice. You begin to start thinking about this in a new light.

I want to extend profound congratulations for breaking the mold to become the best version of yourself. To recognize when something, even in small doses, isn't right and shouldn't be there. The good news, it's all doable! You can reframe your thinking and habits to form new ones around alcohol.

Key Takeaways:

- Alcohol consumption ranges from abstainers/healthy drinkers to severe alcohol use disorders (AUD).
- In-between drinkers exist between moderate drinking and severe AUD.
- Behavioral characteristics include inconsistency, ambivalence, functioning, and control, with no severe consequences.
- A variety of patterns with in-between drinking make it hard to define.
- Society often labels people as either alcoholic or normal.
- In-between drinkers challenge binary views and may struggle to find a clear path to change their relationship with alcohol.
- Reframing thinking and habits can help in-between drinkers make better choices.

Willpower

"We are what we repeatedly do. Excellence, then, is not an act, but a habit."

- ARISTOTLE.

In my journey to change my relationship with alcohol, I discovered that willpower alone was not enough to make lasting changes in habits. I've been socially outgoing most of my life but can also be introverted. Alcohol helped me overcome it early on and became part of my social ritual, particularly during adolescence and young adulthood. As I moved from my 20s into my 30s, my priorities shifted towards family and success rather than socializing or spending evenings at the bar.

The problem was I associated quitting alcohol with giving up fun, and I feared losing my title as the life of the party and giving up enjoyable vacations and nights out. My flexible work schedule involved working online for only 10-15 hours a week, which meant that any night could feel like a Friday, with no need to be at an office the next day.

I established an unhealthy pattern of indulging in evening drinks in this lifestyle. This period was the peak of when I was drinking. It wasn't every night, but it was most nights. To clarify, I never drank during the day and didn't enjoy the sensation of drinking for extended periods. However, I eagerly anticipated my evening wine – and in considerable quantities. A single glass didn't hit the spot after a long day; I preferred nearly a bottle, sometimes even more.

So, I decided to take an extended break, which I did several times. Using willpower alone, I would stop drinking for weeks, sometimes months, and longer. But eventually, since I relied on willpower, I felt I was depriving myself of something, and I would subsequently lose that will. Nothing crazy, but nonetheless, breaking my commitment. Travel, events, and challenging workdays seemed to justify drinking, and I had no structure or framework. As an entrepreneur, there were no defined work hours, so the only way I knew how to tell myself it was time to stop was by pouring that first glass. I would slip back into my old habits. Each time I broke that commitment, it gave me the sense that I was weak, which also broke down my confidence. The truth is, I demonstrated a brute force of will and strength to do it that way. But willpower's mirage will make you think you're weak or flawed.

What I know now, and that studies back up, is that willpower is like a muscle that can become fatigued when overused. This phenomenon, referred to as "ego depletion," suggests that self-control and willpower draw from a limited pool of mental resources. When we deplete these resources, our self-control diminishes, making it more difficult to resist temptations and make decisions aligned with our goals. When it comes to alcohol, relying on willpower alone can lead to a constant battle with oneself, which is why I had difficulty sustaining long-term change.

Because I was having a tough time, I even questioned whether I was an alcoholic. So, I took a simple five questions online assessment, which labeled me an alcoholic. It also labeled my partner Priscilla one, and she only drinks very socially. We didn't agree that I was an alcoholic and needed something like rehab or AA with the labels or the admission of powerlessness.

It wasn't until I reframed in my mind that I was not giving up but instead gaining much more. I then aligned that with a framework of planning and techniques that I achieved lasting change without the need to rely on willpower. I also learned I could apply these concepts beyond alcohol. Changing my diet, stopping procrastination, changing my behaviors in my relationships – they all need more intention than willpower alone.

Unsure of how to create lasting change, I dove into research. When I research something, I go all in. I read every book on addressing alcohol and psychological journals on the subject. I also studied habit change and our mental wiring at a physical and chemical level. This research was invaluable but only took me so far. During this time, I began to have a breakthrough about why I failed to make lasting changes. I reframed my relationship with alcohol, identified my motivations and habits, and developed methods to cope with those behaviors and create new habits.

I became a guinea pig in my research and experimentation. I enlisted my friend Dr. Terranella, a naturopathic doctor, to learn about supplements that could relieve urges and side effects while quitting alcohol. I tried several of these options and documented my experience.

My journey to understand and change my relationship with alcohol involved trial and error, self-reflection, research, persistence, and learning from my failures. I was compelled as an in-between drinker to write this book to share my experiences and knowledge in hopes of helping others struggling with similar issues. I want to pass on the information I wish I had over ten years ago when starting my journey to the greatest version of myself. In writing this book, my primary goal is to guide you in overcoming the struggles I faced with drinking, such as reliance on willpower and self-doubt. By sharing my experiences and knowledge, I hope to help you achieve success in addressing your relationship with alcohol, empowering you to embrace a brighter, more confident future and fully realize your full potential.

Key Takeaways:

- Willpower alone is insufficient for lasting habit changes.
- Extended breaks from alcohol using willpower led to eventual relapse.
- Willpower can become fatigued, leading to self-control challenges.
- Researched habit change, mental wiring, and supplements to aid in quitting.
- Documented personal journey, including trials and errors, to help others.
- Wrote book to share experiences and knowledge for in-between drinkers.

70/20/10

"Beneath the facade of the obvious often lies the essence of the unexpected."

- MIKE HARDENBROOK

I discovered something noteworthy in my research. The moderate drinker category is much smaller than you probably imagined. The top 10% of drinkers account for an eye-opening 50% of the alcohol consumed (Cook, P. J. (2007).

We need to recognize that the alcoholic beverage industry is the primary promotor of the narrative to normalize drinking. The marketing machine targets this message to a small percentage of drinkers who account for a large portion of their profits. Let's examine the data to understand better what this means. Contrary to popular belief, most of the population doesn't drink regularly. About 70% of people are non-drinkers or occasional drinkers. That leaves roughly 20% as moderate drinkers and 10% as heavy drinkers, with some overlap between categories. We need to recognize that not everyone drinks, and many people who do drink do so only occasionally. Financial motives drive this skewed perception of what's "healthy." The alcohol industry promotes the idea that drinking is a normal part of everyday life—not out of safety concerns but to maintain profits.

The alcohol industry knows that 30% of the population generates most of the profits. I'm not one to create or spread conspiracy theories. I'm certainly not in the boardrooms of these companies. However, if we look at the facts, we can see that the industry's marketing tactics heavily influence the societal narrative around alcohol. They target the top 10% of drinkers who generate 50% of the profits, totaling $1.2 trillion worldwide and $234 billion in the United States. That's much higher than the tobacco, pharmaceutical, and illegal drug industries. It's big business with a significant agenda to keep profits flowing.

The health implications of this are significant. The normalization of drinking contributes to various alcohol-related health issues, from physical to mental health. Yet, the alcohol industry often downplays these risks in their marketing, instead focusing on the perceived benefits of alcohol consumption, such as relaxation and social connection.

The societal impacts are also considerable. Alcohol consumption is a factor in many accidents, acts of violence, and other social problems. Yet, the alcohol industry's marketing often associates alcohol with positive experiences, such as celebration and relaxation, rather than the potential negative consequences.

The marketing tactics employed by the alcohol industry are often subtle yet incredibly powerful. They cleverly associate alcohol consumption with positive experiences and emotions, such as relaxation, fun, and social connection. These messages are pervasive in advertisements, movies, music, and social media. Over time, this constant exposure shapes our beliefs and attitudes towards alcohol, making it seem harmless and even necessary in our lives.

The industry also exploits our natural desire for social acceptance and belonging. They promote the idea that drinking is a social activity and that consuming alcohol can enhance our social interactions and make us more likable and accepted by our peers. They make holiday-themed drinks to associate their product with a given holiday. You see this in the commercials, where everyone laughs at a party with a drink. This is particularly concerning as it can lead to peer pressure and normalizing excessive drinking, especially among young people. I know it played a role growing up for me.

For instance, the omnipresence of alcohol advertising can be subtly influential. Seeing alcohol logos on race cars or billboards during our daily commute not only normalizes alcohol but associates it with speed, excitement, and a busy lifestyle. Celebrity endorsements on TV or social media subtly suggest that drinking a particular brand of alcohol is glamorous and a status symbol. Sponsored posts on social media further reinforce this by integrating alcohol into desirable lifestyles and aspirational content. Alcohol promotions in restaurants can make us feel that a meal is incomplete without alcohol. At concerts, sporting events, or festivals, the association of alcohol with fun, entertainment, and relaxation reinforces this concept. Product placements in movies and TV shows can subconsciously influence our choices by making a particular brand seem popular or preferred by characters we admire.

Not many of us watch live TV anymore, but we can all remember a Super Bowl ad that goes to this effect. The commercial features a group of friends enjoying a day at the beach, playing volleyball, swimming, and drinking the advertised brand of beer. The sun shines, everyone laughs, and the scene epitomizes the perfect summer day. The message is clear: fun, sun, friends, and this particular beer brand are all essential ingredients for a good time. The commercial is expertly crafted, with catchy music, beautiful scenery, and attractive actors, all designed to create a positive association with the brand. It is hard not to desire that lifestyle and, by extension, for that beer brand.

TV commercials are a prominent form of marketing, but let's look at some instances where we may not even realize what is happening. One example is the use of nostalgia marketing. For instance, a beer company might release a limited edition can featuring artwork from a popular 80s or 90s TV show or movie. This creates nostalgia in us, as we have fond memories of that time. We might purchase the product not necessarily because we want the beer but because we have positive associations with the imagery on the packaging. This tactic capitalizes on our existing emotional connection to something unrelated to the product.

Another tactic that we might not be aware of is the use of emotional storytelling. Alcohol brands often create commercials that tell a story that evokes strong emotions in us. For example, a commercial might show a father and son bonding over a beer after a long estrangement or friends reuniting and celebrating with a bottle of wine. The story might not have anything to do with the alcohol itself, but it creates a strong emotional response that we associate with the brand. The positive feelings towards the brand are not necessarily because of the product itself but because of the emotions evoked by the story told in the commercial.

To give you an idea, here are even more ways we are impacted daily by alcohol advertising:

Digital Media: Banner ads for a new cocktail on our favorite recipe blogs.
Influencer Partnerships: A popular travel blogger posting a photo with a branded glass of wine at a sunset beach location.
Product Placement: The main character in a popular TV series always drinks the same brand of beer.

Sponsoring Events: A famous music festival sponsored by a vodka brand, with their logos everywhere.

Interactive Advertising: An online game where the characters collect bottles of branded liquor for points.

Brand Collaborations: Limited edition sneakers released in partnership with a tequila brand.

Point-of-Sale Advertising: Special displays and promotions at the liquor store for a particular brand of rum.

Merchandising: T-shirts and caps with a beer brand's logo.

Public Relations: A wine company sponsoring a charity event and getting mentioned in all press releases and interviews.

Guerilla Marketing: Street artists create a mural featuring a whiskey bottle.

Direct Mail: Receiving a postcard in the mail advertising a new craft beer.

Contests and Sweepstakes: Entering a competition to win a trip sponsored by a beer brand.

Word-of-mouth: A friend recommending a new gin they tried at a party.

Loyalty Programs: Collecting points every time we purchase a particular brand of champagne, which can be redeemed for rewards.

Branded Content: A cooking show featuring recipes with a specific red wine brand.

Experiential Marketing: A pop-up bar in the city center created by a cocktail brand.

Celebrity Endorsements: A famous actor appearing in a commercial for a scotch brand.

Affiliate Marketing: A food blogger receives a commission for every sale made through the link they shared for a liquor delivery service.

You can see the marketing is almost everywhere we turn in our daily lives. However, this impact is not uniform across all demographics. Different groups, such as women, older adults, or cultural groups, may be affected differently by the alcohol industry's marketing tactics. For example, some advertisements may target women by associating alcohol consumption with empowerment or independence. Others may target older adults by associating alcohol with relaxation or nostalgia. It is essential to be aware of these targeted marketing tactics and consider how they may influence your perceptions and behaviors.

The policy implications of this are significant. Regulations that limit the alcohol industry's ability to market their products, particularly to vulnerable groups, could help to counteract their influence. Public health campaigns that provide accurate information about the risks of alcohol consumption and promote healthy alternatives can also help to reframe the societal narrative around alcohol.

I aim to empower you with this knowledge to reframe your perception of alcohol based on data rather than marketing. If you're reading this book, you are likely in that 20% category of moderate to moderate-heavy drinkers. While defining these categories can be complex, it's essential to recognize where you stand and the risk of moving into higher-risk categories later in life. By being aware of these statistics, we can better understand our relationship with alcohol and resist social influences and marketing messaging surrounding alcohol.

Key Takeaways:

- The in-between drinker category is less than imagined.
- The top 10% of drinkers consume 50% of alcohol.
- Marketing pushes the moderation narrative for profits.
- Data breakdown: 70% non/light drinkers, 20% moderate, 10% heavy.
- The alcohol industry heavily influences our societal narrative.
- Reframe your perception with data, not marketing.
- Most readers are likely in the moderate or moderate-heavy category with a significant risk of moving into higher-risk categories.

Dopamine Impact

"Dopamine is like a spotlight that focuses on whatever
we're interested in."

- DANIEL G. AMEN.

Even though alcohol is accepted in our society and completely legal, we should realize that alcohol is an addictive substance that affects our brains and drives our behaviors. By understanding what's going on physically, we can better understand why we may behave the way we do, even at what we perceive as moderate quantities that impact our brains.

I intend to give you information to encourage you to review your relationship with alcohol and change your behaviors if needed. As I mentioned, alcohol is addictive for many. This fact is hard to accept, given our programming around alcohol. In the following chapter, I will use alcohol and other drugs to exemplify this reality.

The notion of trying to control your relationship around an addictive substance seems counterintuitive, and in fact, it is. It sounds ridiculous to have a healthy relationship with something like heroin. In a transferable way, we are asking the same from ourselves with alcohol. The comparisons, of course, are extreme. The effects of the two are vastly different socially and physically. But they both have addictive qualities that affect the brain to overuse and form unhealthy habits. So, let's then examine the neuroscience as to why this occurs.

Dopamine is the feel-good chemical released in the brain, which plays a significant role in how we feel on a given day. The measurement of nanograms per deciliter, NPD, will demonstrate these fluctuations.

So, on our typical given day, we produce a range of about 50 NPD, enough energy to get out of bed, start your day, grab a coffee, and feel normal. Now let's look at your worst day when you feel depleted and unable to get going. You may even call in to work and take a sick day. Your worst day level would sit in the range of 40 NPD.

Your best day could be when you are on vacation at your dream spot. You wake up to view crystal-clear water on the beach in front of your villa. And you just got the news of a promotion at work. The range for these two experiences puts you at about 100 NPD. Our brains are meant to operate in this healthy range of 40 to 100 NPD. Forty on our worst day and 100 on our best day –dopamine is not meant to go above this level in a healthy natural state. You would see an increase in dopamine with your favorite food and sex, both produce increases in dopamine in the nineties of NPD.

Now let's look at what happens to dopamine levels. With the introduction of addictive drugs and alcohol, methamphetamines produce massive spikes in dopamine. We see a 10X production in dopamine that pushes the levels above 1000 NPD when marijuana, heroin, and even alcohol is consumed. These are not dopamine levels that our bodies produce naturally. While these spikes in dopamine levels are shocking, why do these numbers matter? When we get these spikes in dopamine that make us feel good beyond typical producing amounts, we find less joy in commonly occurring events. What was once enjoyable, such as a birthday party or hiking, starts to pale compared to the effect of consuming these substances. Of course, we have more extremes with other illicit drugs, but the same occurs with more moderate amounts of alcohol.

The mind also uses dopamine at our primal level to survive. Our ancestors used this as a survival method to provide essentials like food and water. Anyone reading this book is nowhere near these extreme levels, but we must understand the extreme example to see how alcohol and other drugs impact our behaviors. Anyone who becomes substance dependent will react when it is taken away. The first reaction produces a craving. With severe drug addiction, the brain moves into survival mode when that craving is not immediately satisfied. Addicts resort to primal actions by listening to the brain in survival mode. I use this example to show how strongly cravings can drive behaviors. It also explains why people do things they would never do, such as stealing from family or others.

Now, you may think, okay, I drink, but I don't do drugs. I thought the same. Fascinating studies show that alcohol can profoundly affect our cravings. In a study of functional MRI, participants who drank or used to drink were asked, "Tell us about the first time you had a drink and the last time you had a drink." The parts of the brain responsible for inducing cravings lit up. Interestingly, the researchers observed that those parts of the brain lit up almost the same for people who had abstained for 30 days, 90 days, or even a year. It wasn't until two years of abstinence that the signal in the brain began to reduce. Even more interesting was researchers replicated the study around food and water. Subjects were deprived of water or food. The brain's cravings area lit up when the participants were given images of water and food smells.

This example illustrates the power triggers have on our physical minds. Speaking in comparative terms, the activation in the brain for food was about the size of a baseball, while for water, it was the size of a basketball. For alcohol, the activation was akin to the size of a baseball field. The silver lining is that your relationship with alcohol likely isn't at that extreme stage, meaning it won't require drastic measures. While the example is incredibly insightful, it is particularly relevant to those with deep-seated addictions. It demonstrates the level of craving intensity experienced by individuals who have a prolonged history of alcohol consumption. Fortunately, for those of us who are 'in-between' drinkers, the effects are likely shorter and less intense. Our brains' response to triggers will not be as strong as in the case of someone who has been heavily drinking for years. This is a crucial distinction for us to make as it underlines that while alcohol can strongly affect our brains, the level of impact varies significantly based on our drinking habits.

My goal is to highlight how addictive chemicals can profoundly impact our mind and, consequently, our behaviors. We must recognize why we experience cravings and why we may rationalize attending a party as an excuse to indulge. Understanding the science behind our actions equips us with the knowledge to make better-informed decisions.

Overview:

- Alcohol is an addictive substance that impacts the brain and behaviors.
- Dopamine, a feel-good chemical, fluctuates based on mood and experiences.
- Your natural dopamine range is 40-100 NPD.
- Addictive substances elevate dopamine levels beyond the natural range.
- Consequences reduce enjoyment in everyday activities.
- Primal survival: dopamine drives cravings and behaviors.
- Study: alcohol cravings persist for up to two years of abstinence.
- Goal: to understand addiction's impact on our brain and behavior to make informed decisions.

PART

02

Habit Science

"The secret of change is to focus all your energy not on fighting the old, but on building the new."

- SOCRATES.

| Your Commitment Starts Here

Understanding the science behind habit formation is critical to your success in reshaping your habits around your alcohol use. If moderation is your goal, you must abstain for 66 days for several reasons. Moderation requires much more decision-making. For example, "I'll commit to only having two to three. I will only drink on the weekends. I won't drink liquor or wine, only beer. I'll only drink outside of the house." These are too difficult to navigate. Instead, the commitment to abstain for 66 days is a yes or no decision. Later, when patterns are broken and replaced with new habits, you can decide to reintroduce alcohol or choose to abstain. You may wonder why a random number of 66 days. Psychological studies on breaking habits suggest 66 days of abstinence.

If you are like me, you'd think two things. Why the random 66 days, and why so long? 66 days is a significant commitment. My answer to these questions is simple: scientific studies support this number. I will provide you with a framework that breaks the 66 days into increments shortening the commitment. This journey will facilitate a significant positive shift.

Zooming out to view the entirety of your life and efforts puts 66 days in perspective. Would you go for it if you could start a successful business in 66 days? It's interesting how we assign timelines to specific achievements. In our case, I promise better sleep, relationships, less anxiety, better cognition, and unlocking your full potential in just 66 days. To many of you reading this, this is a doable commitment. For those who still feel like it's a long timeline, let's dive into the reasons for using this number.

In the best-selling book *Atomic Habits,* James Clear discusses several studies on healthy habit formation. These studies suggest a much different timeline around habits compared to what has been published by the self-help community over the last 50 years. Let's look into the source of these findings and why I suggest we alter our timeline expectations for creating healthy habits.

In the 1950s, a plastic surgeon, Dr. Maxwell Maltz observed that when he performed operations altering a patient's appearance, it took about 21 days for participants to become accustomed to their new reality (Maltz, 1960). Similarly, patients who had limbs amputated sensed a phantom limb for approximately 21 days before adjusting to their new situation.

These experiences led Dr. Maltz to explore the relationship between these patient observations and human behavior, specifically regarding habit formation. In 1960, his best-selling book *Psycho-Cybernetics: A New Way to Get More Living Out of Life* (Maltz, 1960) sold 30 million copies and became a classic in the self-help genre.

It's important to note that his observations were not part of a controlled study. Maltz focused on patients' physical symptoms, not their human behavior. His findings drew parallels and assumptions about habit formation, citing 21 days as the required time. Others who have reported Maltz's conclusions suggest that he used the minimum number to make goals seem more attainable for readers. Thus, it's essential to approach these widely cited habit formation studies critically, recognizing that the truth may be more nuanced than the popularized 21 to 30-day timeframe.

Another study often cited in connection with habit formation involved NASA astronauts wearing reverse convex goggles that inverted their visual perception. The astronauts' vision adapted after 26 to 30 days, and they could see normally even with goggles. This study confirmed that it takes about 30 days for the brain to rewire and form a new habit. However, there are some surprising flaws with these conclusions. After searching the NASA database, I could not find any documentation of a NASA study on habit formation to support this claim.

Let's focus on a more recent study in a controlled environment on habit formation led by Phillippa Lally, a health psychology researcher at University College London. The study (Lally et al., 2009) monitored the habits of 96 people over 12 weeks. Participants chose one new habit to practice for 12 weeks. These new habits ranged from cutting back on alcohol to fitness challenges and various reward-seeking behaviors. Participants recorded whether they performed the behavior and how automatic it felt.

At the end of the 12 weeks, Lally's team analyzed the data, searching for patterns that would reveal how long it took for individuals to adopt new behaviors and when they became more automatic. They discovered that the participants, on average, took two months for their behaviors to become habits. To be more precise, the data revealed that it took an average of 66 days for new habits to form (Lally et al., 2010). Of course, this timeline varies depending on the individual, behavior, environment, circumstances, and difficulty level. Factoring in this variation, the research found that establishing a new habit takes anywhere from 18 to 254 days (Lally et al., 2010). This finding suggests that we need to be more realistic about the time it takes to change our behaviors. While it's not impossible to form a habit in 21 days, it's certainly improbable. A more accurate outlook is that building new habits could take two to eight months.

Lally's research supports our 66 days starting point for success as a solid foundation. We aim to reframe your expectations surrounding habits. We'll implement a strategy to break up the 66 days incrementally, along with a structure that accommodates slip-ups without needing to start over from scratch. We'll dive deeper into this action plan later in the book. For now, I ask that you consider the data and remain open to embracing the 66 days as a baseline for creating a significant, positive shift in your life. Are you with me? Excellent! Let's continue moving forward on this transformative journey.

Overview:

- Moderation vs. abstinence: 66 days needed for habit change
- Abstaining for 66 days: more straightforward decision-making process
- 66 days: based on Lally's and other psychological studies for habit formation
- Dr. Maxwell Maltz: observed 21 days for patients to adapt to changes
- NASA study: flawed and unsupported, debunked
- Timeframe varies: 18 to 254 days for habit formation
- Incremental approach: accommodates slip-ups without starting over
- Goal: create a significant positive shift in life

Habit Spectrum

"The chains of habit are too weak to be felt until they are too strong to be broken."

- SAMUEL JOHNSON.

In the previous chapter, we covered the Lally study and the principle of 66 days as a baseline for forming new habits. This principle holds, but it's important to understand that not all habits are created equal. Habit lay in a spectrum. The time it takes to form a habit can range widely based on its complexity and the individual in question. Let's break them down into three categories to better understand and identify how they are woven in our daily lives.

Simple Habits: These are actions that almost become second nature and require minimal thought or effort. Think of making your bed each morning or turning off lights when leaving a room. For the majority of us, such habits can be established within the 18 to 66-day range, as proposed by Lally's research.

Moderate Habits: A step above in complexity, these habits necessitate more mindfulness. Committing to a daily 30-minute walk or choosing to prepare a wholesome meal at home instead of opting for fast food are examples. Due to the increased effort and conscious choice involved, these habits might require or stretch beyond the average 66-day threshold for some.

Complex Habits: Here, we're talking about significant lifestyle changes. Maybe it's training for an ultramarathon or dedicating oneself to learning a new musical instrument. The nature of these habits means they demand a combination of mental and physical effort, extended planning, and profound dedication. It wouldn't be surprising if they range between the 66 and 254-day limit mentioned in the Lally study.

So, where does alcohol fit into this spectrum? Alcohol consumption, for many, transcends the simplicity of drinking a morning glass of water. It's nestled somewhere between a moderate and complex habit, especially when we examine the factors influencing our consumption.

For starters, the physiological dimension is essential. Regular drinking can lead to increased tolerance, meaning the body gets accustomed to higher alcohol levels to achieve the same effect. This physical aspect often intertwines with the psychological, making the act of drinking not merely a choice but a craving.

The social aspects in which alcohol is connected with complicate matters. Western cultures view alcohol as a centerpiece of celebration, relaxation, or even commiseration. Its presence is ubiquitous – from festive holidays, birthdays, weddings to casual after-work meetups. This omnipresence means that the habit of drinking is not solely about personal choice but often becomes a communal expectation.

Then there's the emotional aspect. For numerous individuals, alcohol morphs into an emotional crutch, an escape from stress, anxiety, or sadness. This relationship deepens the habit, binding it not only to physiological needs but emotional ones.

Another consideration is the neural pathways being formed. Engaging repeatedly in a habit, like drinking, reinforces specific neural tracks in the brain. The habit then becomes increasingly automatic, a default setting. Breaking or altering these patterns presents more complexity.

It's likely you're somewhere in the moderate to heavy drinking category, seeking a clearer understanding of change. The interplay between simple, moderate, and complex habits, and where alcohol fits into that, is important for us to understand.

In the end, the relationship one has with alcohol is deeply personal, influenced by a variety of factors from one's upbringing, social environment, personal experiences, and even genetics. While the 66-day principle provides a foundation, each of our journeys is unique. Embrace the journey with its ups and downs, always aiming for progress and well-being over rigid timelines. Remember, the journey of changing one's habits, especially around something as potent as alcohol, is as much about self-discovery as it is about self-discipline.

Overview:

- Habit complexity: simple, moderate, and complex habits
- Simple habits: minimal effort, quicker to form (18-66 days)
- Moderate habits: more effort, conscious decision-making, may take longer than 66 days
- Complex habits: significant effort, planning, and dedication could take up to 254 days
- Alcohol as a habit: moderate to complex, influenced by social, emotional, and physiological factors
- Factors affecting resistance to change: personality traits, emotional connections, social influence, previous attempts
- Unique experiences: individual timelines may differ from the 66-day principle
- Focus on progress, not perfection, and be patient with yourself

Brain Circuitry

"The brain is wider than the sky."

- EMILY DICKINSON.

In our journey to reshape our habits with alcohol, it's essential to have a solid understanding of the brain regions involved in habit formation and control. By exploring the basal ganglia, prefrontal cortex, and amygdala, we can gain valuable insights into breaking unwanted habits and develop strategies to support lasting change.

The Basal Ganglia: Habit Formation Central

The basal ganglia, a region deep within the brain, is critical in forming and reinforcing habits. When we repeatedly engage in a particular behavior, such as having a glass of wine after work, the neural pathways in the basal ganglia become activated and strengthened. Over time, this behavior becomes ingrained as a habit, requiring a less conscious effort to initiate and maintain.

Understanding the function of the basal ganglia is critical to reshaping our habits around alcohol. By intentionally interrupting these neural pathways and creating new ones through alternative behaviors, we can begin to establish healthier patterns.

Imagine Samantha, who has developed a habit of pouring herself a glass of wine when she gets home from work. Over time, this behavior has become automatic, with the neural pathways in her basal ganglia being repeatedly activated and strengthened. Sarah creates a new routine to break this habit by walking immediately after work, consciously activating different neural pathways in her basal ganglia, and eventually forming a healthier habit.

The Prefrontal Cortex: Decision-Making and Impulse Control

The prefrontal cortex, located at the front of the brain, is responsible for decision-making and impulse control. When it comes to breaking habits,

the prefrontal cortex plays a vital role in overriding the auto
that drive our actions.

However, breaking habits can be challenging precisely
become automatic, making it difficult for the prefrontal cortex
By increasing our awareness of triggers and consciously e
prefrontal cortex, we can make more deliberate choices that support our
goal of reshaping our relationship with alcohol.

The Battle at Happy Hour

Consider Tom, who struggles to resist alcohol during happy hours with his
coworkers. His prefrontal cortex is responsible for decision-making and
impulse control. Still, the ingrained habit of ordering a beer during these
social gatherings makes it difficult for his prefrontal cortex to intervene.
To override this automatic behavior, Tom consciously engages his
prefrontal cortex by deliberately ordering a non-alcoholic beverage
instead.

The Amygdala: Emotions and Habits

The amygdala, an almond-shaped region in the brain, is responsible for
emotional processing. Emotions are deeply intertwined with habits. Our
actions are connected to specific feelings, making them harder to break.
For example, if we've formed a habit of enjoying a drink to unwind after a
stressful day, the amygdala associates the relief and relaxation with alcohol
consumption. To break this habit, we need to recognize the emotional
connection and develop alternative strategies to cope with stress, such as
exercise, meditation, or engaging in a hobby.

The Emotional Connection to Alcohol

Picture Emily who has developed a habit of drinking alcohol to cope with
stress and negative emotions. Her amygdala has created a strong emotional
connection between alcohol and feelings of relief and relaxation. To break
this habit, Emily must address the emotional aspect of her relationship with
alcohol. She begins practicing yoga and meditation to help manage her
stress and gradually replaces the emotional connection between alcohol
and relaxation with healthier alternatives.

ppose you took all that in and can't get a quick gist. Here's what you need to know:

Basal ganglia: Habit center
Prefrontal cortex: Decision maker
Amygdala: Emotion processor

By understanding the roles of the basal ganglia, prefrontal cortex, and amygdala in habit formation and control, we can develop targeted strategies to reshape our habits around alcohol. With this knowledge, we can be more aware of our triggers, engage in conscious decision-making, and address the emotional aspects of our habits. This holistic approach will support our journey toward a healthier, more balanced relationship with alcohol.

Overview:

- Brain regions involved in habit formation and control: basal ganglia, prefrontal cortex, and amygdala
- Basal ganglia: critical for forming and reinforcing habits
- Interrupting and creating new neural pathways: a key to reshaping habits
- Increasing awareness and engaging the prefrontal cortex: important for breaking habits
- Amygdala: processes emotions and their connections to habits.
- Addressing emotional aspects: essential for breaking habits tied to emotions
- Holistic approach: understanding brain regions, addressing triggers, and emotional aspects for lasting change in alcohol habits.

The Habit Loop

"I am not a product of my circumstances. I am a product of my decisions."

- STEPHEN COVEY.

Let's observe the neuroscience behind the powerful habit loop of cue, routine, and reward. By understanding this loop, we can make meaningful changes in our lives. Though our primary focus is on habits in general, this knowledge will come in handy when we discuss taking a break from alcohol later in the book. So, what exactly is the habit loop? In simple terms, it's a three-step process that our brains use to automate behaviors. It consists of the following:

Cue: The trigger that initiates the habit.
Routine: The behavior or action we perform
Reward: The positive outcome or reinforcement we receive for completing the action.

Our brains have developed a neat trick to make our lives more efficient. Neuroscience has shown that habits are centered around a part of the brain called the basal ganglia. If you recall from the previous chapter, this structure plays a crucial role in our ability to learn, remember, and automate behaviors. The habit loop helps us conserve mental energy by allowing our brains to run on autopilot for routine tasks.

Researchers have found that understanding and manipulating the habit loop can lead to successful habit change (Duhigg, 2012). Focusing on the cue, routine, and reward allows us to rewire our brains to adopt or modify new or existing habits. Keep in mind that the success rate varies from person to person, as individual factors such as motivation, consistency, and support systems come into play. Now, let's break down each component of the habit loop:

The Cue is a signal or trigger that tells our brains to initiate a specific habit. A cue can be external, like a particular time of day or location, or internal, like a specific emotion or thought. Identifying the cue is crucial for understanding the habit loop and changing our behavior.

The Routine is the behavior or action in response to the cue. Routines can be simple, like grabbing a snack when you're hungry, or more complex, like running after work to unwind. The key is that the routine becomes automatic over time as our brains associate the cue with the action.

The Reward is the positive reinforcement we receive after completing the routine. It can be something tangible, like the taste of a favorite snack, or intangible, like the sense of accomplishment after a workout. The reward reinforces the habit loop, making it more likely that we'll repeat the behavior.

Now, let's explore further the Reward phase of the habit loop. At its core, each habit we cultivate often pursues a specific desired outcome. Our brain doesn't adopt routines randomly; it embraces habits that consistently lead to rewards or outcomes that meet our needs or desires. This outcome is essentially the brain's way of validating the efficiency of the habit loop: we reinforce the loop if a routine results in a desired reward.

The math is straightforward when thinking about the relationship between a desired outcome and the likelihood of that outcome occurring. If the probability of achieving the desired reward after a routine is high, our brain views the habit as highly efficient, strengthening it. In many ways, this efficiency is akin to an investment with an almost guaranteed return, and our brains, always seeking optimization, are eager investors.

Let's examine this in the context of alcohol. The primary goal or desired outcome of consuming alcohol is to feel better or relieve pain. Whether it's the stress from a hard day's work, a coping mechanism for personal issues, or the desire to get a buzz, the outcome is clear: relief or pleasure.

When you drink alcohol, the outcome - that feeling of relief or pleasure - is almost certain. The near 100% probability makes the habit loop around alcohol compelling. It's hard to break a habit that consistently delivers on its promise with a perfect record. In this sense, alcohol is one of the brain's most "efficient" habits, at least from the perspective of desired outcomes.

Think about it. You've had a taxing day. The cue might be your emotional exhaustion as you step through your front door. The routine is heading straight to the refrigerator or cabinet, pulling out that bottle, and pouring yourself a drink. Then comes the reward: that immediate sensation of relaxation, the melting away of stress, the euphoric buzz, or even the taste. This is your brain's desired outcome, and given that it happens nearly every time, the loop strengthens, embedding the habit deeper into your psyche.

While the short-term desired outcome is consistently met, the long-term consequences of this high-efficiency habit loop might not align with your life goals. While our brains are programmed for efficiency, we must remember that they don't always account for the broader picture. That is where the challenge lies. The draw of alcohol, with its almost guaranteed outcome, is powerful. But understanding this allure, the neuroscience behind it, and the broader context is crucial if we ever hope to redirect or modify this habit loop.

So, as we journey forward, remember that we're not just combating a routine or an ingrained habit. We're challenging an efficient system that our brain has perfected over time. But we enable ourselves by acknowledging the desired outcome and its probability, understanding the workings of the habit loop. This knowledge is a tool that can guide us as we navigate the complexities of our relationship with alcohol and other habits.

Overview:

- Neuroscience of habit loop: cue, routine, reward
- Habits centered around basal ganglia
- The habit loop conserves mental energy
- Manipulating habit loop for successful change
- Cue: external or internal signals
- Routine: automatic behavior or action
- Reward: positive reinforcement
- Habit loop strengthens neural connections

Decision Fatigue

"Decision fatigue helps explain why ordinarily sensible people get angry at colleagues and families, splurge on clothes, buy junk food at the supermarket, and can't resist the dealer's offer to rustproof their new car. No matter how rational and high-minded you try to be, you can't make decision after decision without paying a biological price."

- JOHN TIERNEY.

Understanding the science behind our behavior empowers us to make informed decisions. Now, I'd like to take some time to apply the science to decision fatigue, something long-studied and proven. Decision fatigue is the brain's mental overload that impedes our ability to make good decisions. These factors are directly related to the success of giving up alcohol for a period or for good. Your ability to make good decisions or keep to a commitment lessens – which is why the witching hours get their name and why it can be the most difficult to resist a glass of wine at the end of the day. Relying on willpower alone is generally a strategy that only works for some people.

Chemical Influence on Decision Fatigue: One essential factor is that our brains rely heavily on glucose, its primary energy source. As we make decisions throughout the day, our brains consume this glucose. After a barrage of decisions, our capacity for sound decision-making decreases when glucose runs low. Interestingly, alcohol can further interfere with our glucose metabolism, making the fatigue even more pronounced after consuming it. This adds another layer of complexity to the decision-making process when resisting that drink after a long day of constant decision-making.

The Paradox of Choice: Additionally, our modern era bombards us with endless choices, leading to what's termed "the paradox of choice." This isn't just about making decisions; it's about the exhaustion from having too many options. When surrounded by choices at every corner, even a simple decision like what to drink can be mentally draining. This is why the many choices we face after a tiring day can lead to a mental standstill or regrettable decisions.

We already know that our brains generate cravings that we must resist or manage, and even moderate alcohol consumption can create these cravings. Picture this: you had a wild night out, and the following day, you wake up determined not to drink again, at least not that evening. Each of these situations tests our resolve.

The Role of Emotions: Let's remember the emotional dimension of our decisions. Decision fatigue doesn't only cloud our logical reasoning; it intensifies our emotional reactions. This interplay can be especially noticeable after a long day. Not only are we likely to make poor choices concerning alcohol, but we might also be more susceptible to the emotional pull of a drink. The imagined relaxation it promises or the social bonds it signifies.

To illustrate how decision fatigue impacts our decisions, let's look at some estimated brain activity. In terms of our thought processes, on an average day, we process approximately 60,000 thoughts. Additionally, we engage in an inner monologue at a rate of about 120 words per minute. Various studies also estimate that we make around 35,000 remotely conscious decisions throughout the day. However, it's important to keep in mind that this figure is based on scientific estimates. It's more of a general notion to illustrate the many choices and decisions we face in our daily lives. No wonder we tend to make poor decisions by the end of the day. In my own experience, I start the day with eggs and greens and drink plenty of water. Lunch is lean chicken, olive oil, and a salad combo at dinner time. Even though my resolve to eat clean all day has been strong, I find myself eating foods that break my commitment when ordering out, seeing and smelling the foods on the tables –the images of fried chicken and desserts on the menu–and then ordering unhealthy options. Why is it that all day I could make a healthy dietary decision until dinner? Decision fatigue causes me to break my commitment.

We also may say things we may not usually say. Decision Fatigue is why some couples fight in the evenings when self-control and decisions are at their lowest. So, when it comes to our drinking, we are hit with a double whammy. Science tells us that alcohol produces cravings in the brain and that cravings increase to their highest between 12 to 24 hours from your last drink. So, we already know we have that to overcome. Then, we add 60,000 thoughts per day with 35,000 decisions made over the day. This complexity is why even moderate drinkers need help and why willpower alone is not a strategy for a long-term commitment. Instead, we need a framework when decision-making is at its lowest point. Fortunately, a framework is precisely what we are building on this journey.

Overview:

- Science empowers informed decisions.
- Decision fatigue is defined as mental overload that impacts choices.
- Witching hours: the end of the day, the most challenging time to resist alcohol.
- Willpower alone is insufficient for success.
- Moderate alcohol consumption generates cravings.
- External factors test our resolve.
- Mental energy: 1,250 thoughts per minute, 35,000 daily decisions
- Decision fatigue affects evening choices.
- Double whammy: cravings and decision fatigue
- Moderate drinkers need help.
- Framework needed for low decision-making points

Synaptic Plasticity

*"It is in your moments of decision that your
destiny is shaped."*

- TONY ROBBINS.

In the previous chapters, we explored brain structures like the basal ganglia, prefrontal cortex, and amygdala. We've discovered how the cue-routine-reward cycle integrates with our day-to-day lives, especially in the context of alcohol. Now, let's explore a transformative concept known as synaptic plasticity and how it could be our ally in reshaping our habits.

At its core, synaptic plasticity is the ability of our brain to dynamically adjust the strength and efficiency of connections between neurons or synapses based on our experiences and environmental stimuli. Imagine synaptic connections as pathways in a dense forest. The more often you hike a specific path, the clearer and more established it becomes. In contrast, neglect a trail, and it becomes overgrown and challenging to navigate. This adaptability is pivotal as it enables our brains to adjust to new situations and shapes our habits.

Consider the analogy of a musician, like a pianist learning a piece. The notes might be fumbled, the rhythm off. But with practice, synaptic connections to that piece strengthen, making the music more fluid and instinctual.

So, what does this forest of synaptic pathways have to do with our habits around alcohol? When we repetitively indulge in behaviors like sipping wine, we cement those neural pathways, turning them from dirt trails into superhighways of habit. Over time, as these paths become burned in, they convert into habits.

The silver lining here is the dual nature of synaptic plasticity. It's not only a tool for habit formation; it's also a mechanism for habit change. When we intentionally immerse ourselves in new activities and coping strategies, we can diverge from the established pathways linked to old habits. By doing so, we pave the way for new, healthier routes in our neural forest.

Think about everyday habits many of us share. For example, morning reliance on coffee is a common habit. Many of us wouldn't function without that cup to start the day. But a shift to tea, though challenging initially, gradually restructures the brain's craving. The pathways to coffee weaken, making space for the growing connections to tea drinking.

The power of synaptic plasticity underscores the potential for meaningful habit change. Brown University (Kuhlman et al., 2020) found that a greater understanding of synaptic plasticity mechanisms could improve behavioral interventions. It's a reminder that our brain isn't just a passive observer but an ever-evolving entity, reshaping and refining its connections.

To navigate our relationship with alcohol, an understanding of synaptic plasticity provides us with a roadmap. It's not about willpower; it's about understanding the malleable pathways of our brain. It's about recognizing that with effort, persistence, and knowledge, we can redirect the neural traffic, choosing paths that serve us better.

With this foundation, as we progress through the book, you'll discover that our strategies and insights aren't just pulled from thin air. They're grounded in the intricate neurons in our brain, a testament to their incredible adaptability and resilience.

Overview:

- Synaptic plasticity: the brain's ability to change neuron connections.
- Habits form through synaptic connections.
- Synaptic plasticity helps change the brain to form and break habits.
- Mindfulness practices and habit replacement leverage synaptic plasticity
- Research supports synaptic plasticity for habit change.
- Your understanding of synaptic plasticity is crucial to adapting and adjusting habits.

Neurogenesis & Neuroplasticity

"The brain can be developed just the same as the muscles can be developed if one will only take the pains to train the mind to think."

- THOMAS A. EDISON.

In the previous chapter, we introduced you to the synaptic plasticity and the brain's ability to adapt. Let's explore the concept of adaptability in more detail by discussing neuroplasticity and neurogenesis. We will examine how these concepts contribute to our ability to adapt and learn throughout our lives. The more you understand, the more we can unlock your potential for transforming habits with alcohol.

Our exploration starts with an introduction to the concepts of neuroplasticity. According to Dr. Celeste Campbell (brainline.org), neuroplasticity is "the brain's amazing capacity to change and adapt. It refers to the physiological changes in the brain that happen due to our interactions with our environment. From the time the brain begins to develop in utero until the day we die, the connections among the cells in our brains reorganize in response to our changing needs." This process allows us to learn and adapt to different experiences. It's the power of our brains to rewire themselves to adapt to the ups and downs of life.

Imagine your brain as a city constantly evolving. Just as a city adapts its infrastructure to meet the changing needs of its population, our brains reorganize and construct new neural pathways while discarding dated ones. Neuroplasticity is our brain's urban planner. It ensures our mind remains agile, flexible, and open to new experiences.

Before we go into detail about neuroplasticity, let's revisit the microcosm of synaptic plasticity. Synaptic plasticity focuses on the minute adjustments within our brain's network of neurons. It's the fine-tuning of individual connections, known as synapses, based on how often they are used.

A well-known phenomenon of synaptic plasticity is Long-Term Potentiation (LTP). Repeated stimulation strengthens synaptic connections between neurons, much like when musicians perfect their performance through strict practice. In simpler terms, synaptic plasticity is like fine-tuning individual instruments in an orchestra to ensure harmonious performance. It's the micro-level adaptation that contributes to the symphony of neuroplasticity.

Let's now turn our attention back to how neuroplasticity plays a pivotal role in habit formation. Neuroplasticity, eloquently described by Dr. Alfa Pasqua Leon, can be likened to a snowy hill. Imagine your brain as this snowy hill on a winter's day, waiting to be explored. When you sled down a freshly snowed hill, the path is yours to choose. However, as you continue down that path repeatedly, following the path already taken is more natural. After an afternoon of sledding, those initial paths become deeply ingrained, making them challenging to alter. They're the well-worn grooves created by repeated actions.

Now, consider neuroplasticity as a fresh snowfall on that hill. While the traces of the old paths remain, the new snow offers new possibilities. It's like the slate has been wiped clean, exposing new directions to explore. This metaphor beautifully illustrates how our thought patterns and habits form.

Your brain creates a neural pathway when you repeatedly engage in behavior like drinking wine every night. These pathways become increasingly efficient with each repetition, making the behavior feel automatic and deeply ingrained. Neuroplasticity allows for creating new mental pathways, providing opportunities for change, much like how fresh snowfall can reshape a hill.

The concept of neuroplasticity is scientific proof that we can create new pathways in our minds. Together, we'll explore how to use this power to transform your habits and lead a more fulfilling life.

Let's shift our focus to neurogenesis, a concept that has reshaped our understanding of brain plasticity. Neurogenesis is the process of generating new neurons. Contrary to previous beliefs that neurogenesis was limited to prenatal and early postnatal stages, recent research has illuminated that it can occur in adulthood (Ming & Song, 2011). This breakthrough highlights neurogenesis's critical role in learning, memory, and mood regulation. While neurogenesis alone might not help you quit drinking, it can contribute to overall brain health and improve the effectiveness of other strategies to help you overcome alcohol dependence.

Imagine neurogenesis as the generation of new neurons, the builders of our brain. It's like a city continually constructing new residential or commercial areas to accommodate a growing population. It's believed neurons generate in specific brain regions, such as the hippocampus, even during adulthood. These new neurons integrate into existing neural circuits, enriching the brain's cognitive resources.

Our understanding of the role of neurogenesis becomes particularly important when we consider the impact of alcohol on this process. Chronic alcohol use can impede neurogenesis, disrupting neuron generation and integration.

Diminished neurogenesis can have far-reaching consequences. Compromising cognitive functions may result in difficulty learning, remembering, and adapting. It can also impact our mood regulation and contribute to emotional challenges.

Now that we've explored these concepts let's explore how we can support and stimulate neurogenesis.

Neurogenesis

Exercise: Regular exercise promotes brain health and neurogenesis. Aim for 150 minutes of moderate aerobic activity or 75 minutes of intense activity weekly, plus bi-weekly strength training.

Nutrition: A diet with antioxidants, omega-3s, and brain-boosting nutrients supports neurogenesis. Prioritize whole foods.

Mindfulness & Meditation: These practices enhance neurogenesis, reduce stress, and improve emotional balance, aiding in better alcohol habits.

Sleep: Aim for 7-9 hours nightly, emphasizing quality and consistency, to foster neurogenesis.

Social Connections: Building strong connections benefits brain health and boosts neurogenesis.

Neuroplasticity

Cognitive Stimulation: Activities like puzzles or learning new skills strengthen neural connections and increase neuroplasticity.

Stress Management: Counteract chronic stress by embracing techniques like deep breathing, muscle relaxation, or engaging in enjoyable activities.
Supporting Both Neurogenesis and Neuroplasticity

Psychedelics: Some psychedelics, such as psilocybin found in magic mushrooms, can initiate both neurogenesis and neuroplasticity. However, it's important to seek advice from a healthcare expert and consider participating in a regulated therapeutic environment for their safe use.

As you progress through the chapters, we'll explore in greater detail how to harness the potential of neuroplasticity and neurogenesis into actionable steps. Ultimately, this will be an invaluable lesson for reshaping habits with alcohol.

Overview:

- Neurogenesis: new neuron creation improves learning, memory, and mood.
- Neuroplasticity: reshaping brain pathways like fresh snow on a hill
- Benefits: enhanced learning/memory, mood regulation, cognitive flexibility, reinforcing recovery efforts
- Promote neurogenesis through exercise, nutrition, mindfulness, sleep, cognitive stimulation, social connections, stress management, and supervised use of psychedelics.
- Overall, brain health supports lasting change in alcohol relationships.

Pendulum Theory

*"The only way to make sense out of change is to plunge
into it, move with it, and join the dance."*

- ALAN WATTS.

We constantly switch from one extreme to another our behaviors, habits, and emotions. With emotions, it's common to alternate between pleasure and pain, love and hate, and anger and peace. Let's talk about diet, for example. We regularly see people going on highly restrictive diets, then swinging back to old behaviors and losing resolve. Another example is yo-yo dieting. Your dieting goes up and down from one point to the opposite point, never settling in the middle. Now let's apply this concept in terms of your behaviors around drinking. Before you draw some conclusions, let me state that the equilibrium for drinking is not moderation for everyone and is not a fixed point. I will explain more in this chapter. Keep that in mind as we move forward. But first, let's observe the typical pendulum swing for our drinking.

In this example, we will use our equilibrium, the set standard of moderate drinking in a healthy community. Note: the consensus of 2020 is that alcohol presents no health benefits. So, the idea of healthy moderation is counterintuitive. Nonetheless, we will set a baseline of one to two drinks per day, seven a week, or fourteen a week.

Let's create a hypothetical scenario. You do pretty well with daily moderation. You may go to a party or gathering, but most days, you stay in equilibrium with drinking. However, come Sober October, you decide to abstain for 30 days. So overnight, the weight is pulled to one side of the pendulum.

The first week it takes all your willpower to resist invites to happy hour after work. And on another occasion, you put in 10 hours of work and come home completely deflated. Your partner is sipping a glass of wine with the open bottle on the table. It takes all you have to resist. You even pick the bottle up, smell it, examine it, and read the label. You manage to put it down and watch some TV before bed. On week two, you are feeling good. You're sleeping better, and you feel more relaxed. There's conflict at work, but it's much more manageable. You are feeling more refreshed and centered. However, by week three, you're finding it harder to resist the invitations to happy hour. You decide on day 23 that it's close enough to day 30. You start questioning your decision to abstain and try to convince yourself that depriving yourself of pleasure makes no sense. In this way, you are weighing the extremes of pleasure versus pain on the pendulum.

With no alcohol, the brain has gone from perceived benefit and pleasure to that pain. Resisting and obstructing are now associated with more pain than pleasure. So, the next time you get the happy hour invite, you accept. It is different this time. This time you deserve the reward. You believe you have earned a few more rounds. After five drinks, you head home. Instead of going to bed, you see that wine on the counter and think, why not? I haven't had anything in weeks. Not only have I earned it, but what's the harm?

So now the pendulum has swung back in the other direction. This time it doesn't fall back to equilibrium. Instead, you stay closer or entirely at the extreme side of drinking for a period; it's your time to cut loose. You are free of the restrictions. Been there, done that. So now, as a result, you go out more often. You give less thought about the quantities you drink. There is no consequence. But later, you start waking up groggy, and your moods aren't as balanced. During a presentation, you have a panic attack, and to top it off, you have had a big blow-up with your partner after a few too many. Now what is perceived as the pendulum's state has flipped to pain. So, after experiencing pain, you decide to cut back a few times a week. But all of a sudden, you find that difficult. You don't experience that immediate gratification as before; counting becomes a point of decision fatigue. So, you see, the best way to return to the state of pleasure is to swing back to the other side of the pendulum.

Unfortunately, understanding your behaviors and relying on willpower alone is necessary for you to swing back again, perpetually swinging back and forth –a prevalent theme in many human behaviors. It's not all related to our habits with alcohol. In laying out the scenario, your questioning goes from extreme to extreme. Going to present a recipe for failure is the best equilibrium, one of moderation. The answer to that is a resounding no. The points of the pendulum are not fixed, and over time we can reset the equilibrium to something completely different. The example I gave here set the drink equilibrium of moderation of one to two drinks. Your equilibrium might be four to five. We also set the extremes from zero to six plus. These can be reset and changed over time, and where the 66 days factor in beautifully. The longer you sit at the extreme for 66 days or more, the more extreme the pendulum shifts to the center. It becomes your equilibrium, with old extremes replaced by nuances. Let's observe the visuals by comparison to demonstrate this.

Suppose you abstain from alcohol for 66 days. This duration may vary for different individuals, but let's assume that you have formed a new habit. You have reset the scales. The extreme ends of the pendulum, initially associated with restriction, have now shifted towards equilibrium. The previous extremes have been replaced with new ones: the negative side (drinking) has been replaced with the old equilibrium, and the old average (neutral) has moved to the high end of drinking.

Reintroducing moderation likely won't lead to adverse consequences at this stage because the habit has been broken. Occasional drinks become just that - occasional. It's up to the individual to maintain this consistency and prevent slipping back into old habits. Many people will successfully keep their new habits, but some may face the risk of regression.

Several factors can influence the likelihood of regression, including the duration and intensity of the initial unhealthy relationship with alcohol. There's a difference between a person who didn't have many problems with drinking and someone who has become a heavy drinker over the years or decades. The latter is placed in the category associated with a higher risk of regression. Genetics will have a bearing on this as well. If you have a high rate of alcoholism in your family, that puts you at a higher risk of regressing even if your drinking never reached that level. The environment can also play an impact. Surrounding yourself with others who regularly drink can play a role in your failure. Falling back into new habits by personality will play a role, as well as why you drink. Sometimes it's for fun or social reasons. But many of us use it as a coping mechanism. And unless we address this as the source, these coping mechanisms will have a stronger pull and can increase the likelihood of reintroducing alcohol. Some of these new extremes might represent the current limits, but they could be temporary for some individuals, while the old norms still linger in the background, ready to return.

Here's the good news, most of you in the at-risk categories will likely experience so much benefit by day 66 that reintroducing alcohol in moderation won't even be a consideration. You have erased the perceived benefit and pleasure of alcohol. At this point, you may question if you can reintroduce a healthier relationship with alcohol. Many individuals have achieved this successfully and gone on to longstanding habits. It's up to you what your goal is.

Perhaps your goal is to have better moderation after the 66 days commitment –certainly an attainable goal. It is up to you to be very mindful during the reintroduction period. Observe how it goes. If you sense that you are beginning to swing back to old habits, you return to what you know well: the framework and commitment you made during the 66 days. It's really that simple. You can look at it as an experiment. I bet this isn't your goal by the end of the 66 days, even if it's your goal today. You have made a significant change in your life – a life with mental clarity, better sleep, better sex, low anxiety, and a positive outlook. You'll be hard-pressed to want to depart all of that for a few drinks here and there.

Before writing this book and researching it, I looked at abstinence as a trial-and-error experiment. I have often gone 30 days with the notion that this is required to change a habit. Usually, after that period, I would return to alcohol to reduce and moderate it. We now know that it is not sufficient to form new habits. So, whenever I had a few drinks, it started occasionally for a period. I would have some wine in the evenings. However, I didn't feel good about it in the morning, especially considering how great I had felt during those 30 days. So, the next night was an easy no for a period. It was random. A few drinks here and there. Occasionally, I had drinks at every social event and after work. Old habits die hard, as the saying goes. So, when I found myself there, I would reassess and recommit. Thirty days were not enough for me to form new habits. Additionally, I attribute my long relationship with alcohol since adolescence as a significant factor. Whether to decide on abstinence or moderation, I did not have an answer until I experimented with one that clarified the matter.

The clarity came from an extended break from alcohol. Instead of 30 days, I decided to try 60 days. At that point, I thought 30 days wasn't long enough. I also wanted to challenge myself. No rock bottom or event drove this decision. It was simply a challenge to become the best version of myself. When I reached the 60-day mark, something interesting happened. I made an instant decision and an easy one. Why not go for 90 days? So, I did, and I did it without blinking. At this point, I had solidified the habit. Going from 30 days to 90 days was a cinch. When I reached the 90-day mark, I asked myself, why not keep going? And for ten months, I did just that. Ten months was not as difficult as the first 60 days. In fact, if I were to say on a scale of one to ten, my urge to drink after the first 60 days would sit at around a zero to three out of ten, depending on the day or environment. That's the beauty of making this commitment. It gets easier over time. It becomes automatic. It has become a habit. However, around the ten-month mark, we were traveling as a family, and as we often do, we spent the summer in the downtown Chicago loop. The loop is a fun area with tons of things to do – restaurants, outdoor events, beer, gardens, concerts, and the lakefront. During this time, I would think, "It sure would be nice to have an ice-cold Moscow mule on the river." My environment had reintroduced my association with alcohol. Looking around at everyone else, drinking and laughing, made me wonder if I could have a take-it-or-leave-it attitude now.

At some point, I made a conscious decision to drink. I had not made a commitment to abstain forever. I simply had gone for ten months on autopilot. I did not make an impulsive decision. Instead, I promised to observe closely if my relationship had permanently changed. I had that drink at a riverside bar, and honestly, I remember vividly thinking, "Is this it? Is this what I didn't want to let go?" The drink did very little for me. It didn't taste good, and it wasn't refreshing. I lost my taste for alcohol.

I didn't particularly like drinking anymore. That was my answer. Unfortunately, this awareness didn't last long term. I gave less thought to decision-making in social settings. I accepted drinking as part of going out. Then the occasional drink at home with a movie. Nothing serious, but slowly I shifted back to my old habits. At that point, I had to reassess. I concluded that I had spent the better part of my adolescent and adult life with alcohol at the center of my social life. My timeline was not in my favor. And, more importantly, I used alcohol to cope with stress from a long day, feelings of anxiety, and tune out.

As I mentioned, the ability to return to moderation while keeping new habits intact is highly personal. For me, habits stay intact if I decide to abstain. The good part of this realization is that the desire was easy, given how energized, confident, and happy I was when I made that commitment. Mine is just one story. Your story could play out differently. In fact, it probably will. Exploring and reaching the best version of ourselves is a personal journey. So, move forward in this book with that knowledge, and pay close attention to your motivations and goals.

Keep an open mind that they are fluid goals that can change with clarity and time. Your goal may be to stop for good. That's great. This book will support you on that journey. Maybe your goal is to take a break, reset, and reintroduce alcohol in moderation. That's also an admirable goal. These healthy goals may change during your journey to 66 days. That is entirely normal. There is no right or wrong way. The only thing that you need to do now is to commit to 66 days.

Overview:

- Extreme emotions: pleasure and pain, love and hate, anger and peace.
- Diet: restrictive diets and yo-yo dieting.
- Drinking: pendulum swings between extremes.
- Equilibrium is not fixed; varies for individuals.
- 66 days to reset equilibrium and form new habits.
- Factors affecting regression: duration/intensity of the unhealthy relationship, genetics, environment, coping mechanisms.
- Potential benefits of abstaining from alcohol: mental clarity, better sleep, better sex, low anxiety, and positive outlook.
- Experimenting with abstinence/moderation: author's personal story.
- Individual journey: goals may change during the 66-day process, so keeping an open mind is important.
- Commit to 66 days for a change.

PART

03

External Forces

"The strength we search for externally often flourishes in the silent corners of our inner being."

- MIKE HARDENBROOK.

Cycle Breaking

As you begin this journey, remember you are not weak. You do not possess an addictive personality. Let's address the first point. We already know that alcohol, even in small amounts, is an addictive substance and causes cravings. There is a window for consumed alcohol to process through your body and mind. Breaking the cycle is challenging. New research indicates alcohol recovery can take as long as two weeks. Within that timeline, it can seem worse before it gets better. Your level of drinking and your body's recovery to your natural homeostasis is unique to you. Symptoms that you may experience at the beginning of your journey include mood swings, insomnia, low energy, restlessness, anxiety, and trouble concentrating.

From my experience, I had the most issues with insomnia in the initial phase of giving up alcohol. I could not stay asleep. The good news is I have found supplements that helped me tremendously reduce insomnia and other symptoms. Sleep recharges the mind and body, giving us more substantial willpower. Although using willpower is not part of our framework, it still plays a part in our conviction to stop drinking.

My experience is common for many, but it felt uncommon to me. I now have learned that it is prevalent in people who struggle to quit drinking and have highly demanding jobs. I needed to find something else to replace that destructive habit. Here's how my typical cycle would play out. As an entrepreneur who works from home, I had no defined working time. I didn't know how to shut down at night when I had a very productive and long day at work. The way for me officially to say it was quitting time and to check out was to open that bottle of wine. But one or two, you have a big day tomorrow. What would happen is similar to this scenario. My wife Priscilla and I would put on a movie. She would pour a glass of wine. I would have my limit of two and start feeling good. We love comedies, so we would laugh and have a good time together.

After a long day, my good decision-making is at its lowest. Couple that with some wine, and it's a recipe for broken promises. So, while we are having a good time, the urge to have another seems like a good idea. Why not? What's one more going to hurt? Well, this is the slippery slope. The more you have, the lower the ability to make good decisions. Even though we are having a good time, the decision to have more was not helpful. We have such a good time that we decide to watch something else after the movie after staying up later than needed for a restful sleep.

On top of that, we have a late-night snack, adding to the alcohol calories. Alcohol and food late at night are a recipe for poor-quality sleep. And so, the following day, I woke early as always, but with a dry mouth and feeling exhausted. Not just exhausted but feeling completely wrung out. I take a cold shower to shock myself into being awake, head downstairs to the coffee maker, and drink at least two cups to get myself back to normal. At this point, I am feeling anxious and fearful about what I have to achieve today. I also have regret and self-loathing about breaking my promise of not drinking. In the future, if I decided to drink, I promised myself I would stick to my limit of one to two glasses.

I usually would go to the gym to work up a good sweat hitting the weights and sauna to get myself level. All the while, I am fighting anxiety and brain fog. Working out helped quite a bit. But it didn't remove the regret. Nor did it dismiss my need to feel like I needed to mask my previous night from others. Deep down, I knew I was better than this. The day would go on, and I would usually meet all my expectations at work. But I could not be as productive had I skipped the alcohol and slept well. With time and hydration, I began feeling better as the day went on. By the afternoon, I promised myself I didn't need wine tonight. It's been a rough day, and I don't want that again. But by the evening, that narrative would change to "It's been a hard day; I deserve to relax and feel better." To my wife, "I want to watch a movie and have a glass of wine or two." The cycle would repeat itself.

It's important to note a few reasons this was my story and, to some degree, that of many others. It didn't happen to me every day. When I rationalized my drinking, this scenario typically played out. I didn't quite grasp two things: after a full day of mind-making decisions, a mental and physical reality is that we are much more prone to make poor decisions.

The withdrawal effects of even moderate drinking last around 12 to 24 hours. So chemically, the alcohol was causing cravings that I needed to resist at my lowest state of decision-making. With this reality, we know willpower is not an answer to stopping drinking. It sets us up for failure and makes us feel weak and powerless to stop drinking. Instead, we need to reframe our mindset in these periods and rely on a framework to follow when cravings arise. Time is our most significant ally. The more distance we can put from alcohol, the easier it gets. Once the body releases the physical cravings, breaking and sustaining the habit is much easier.

Overview:

- You're not weak, nor do you have an addictive personality.
- Alcohol is addictive, causing cravings and cycle-breaking.
- Initial alcohol abstinence symptoms: mood swings, insomnia, low energy, anxiety.
- Supplements and techniques reduce symptoms.
- The recovery timeline varies; willpower is not enough.
- Typical cycle: drinking, poor sleep, anxiety, brain fog, promises not to drink, repeat pattern.
- Poor decision-making after a full day; withdrawal effects last 12-24 hours.
- Reframe mindset, use the framework and time as allies for distance from alcohol.

Motivation Discovery

"The only journey is the one within."

- RAINER MARIA RILKE.

The reasons why we drink are very personal. In this chapter, we'll explain why most people drink. I ask you to keep an open mind. One reason is as simple as your environment, for example, social events where it is the norm to join in drinking with others. Later we will peel back a layer to the source of why you drink and why stopping can be challenging. I want to view drinking as a symptom rather than a problem. An unhealthy relationship goes deep.

Let's look at how we interpret anxiety. Generally speaking, when we experience anxiety, we don't blame the anxiety. We trace the source of that anxiety. Typically, we trace it to issues with self-worth, external triggers, or past events that bring up those emotions. Similarly, what is causes you to have a relationship with alcohol that is unhealthy? Why do you rely on alcohol when it no longer serves you?

When I was younger, I drank excessively –in social settings, at parties in high school, and later, in my fraternity at the university. I attributed my drinking to being young, wild, and exploring something new --all true. As an adult, I now realize there were more convincing reasons why I drank at that age. I typically kept my drinking to weekends and never at home.

During years of reflection, I have uncovered why I drank. In my early elementary and junior high years, I was an athlete. I also was outgoing and confident but went to a rough school. I was not immature or gullible. But I also was not one of the cool kids. I experienced a fair amount of bullying. I just dealt with it. I was not a victim, but it shaped how I felt in school and around others. Without realizing it, I developed a sense of rejection. Drinking at parties comforted me and I felt accepted and cool. In high school, I joined in with the partying crowd. I found my new angle to be cool in college. Alcohol suppressed my fears of rejection and reduced my attachments to past adverse events. I didn't view it as a boohoo back then and to this day. I wanted to be young and wild. My drinking was my attempt to cope. Adolescents vary from kids who never drink to those who do, like me. All who drink have reasons beyond the youthful coming of age. Let's take a step back now and examine why you drink. It doesn't have to be some skeleton in the closet. I have none. You want to be aware and mindful of your behaviors to identify underlying motivations.

Motivation is what drives us to pursue a goal. Two factors form the goals you intend to achieve. The formula is **value x likelihood**. Let's dive a bit deeper into this "value x likelihood" equation because it's key to understanding our motivations and behaviors, including those surrounding alcohol.

At its core, every goal we set hinges on these two factors. The value part of the equation refers to the benefit or reward we perceive in achieving that goal. In terms of our relationship with alcohol, we might value it as a stress reliever, a social lubricant, or an escape from our daily troubles.

The likelihood part of the equation is all about our assessment of the odds. Will having a drink actually provide the relief or confidence boost we're seeking? Most of the time, our brains might calculate that yes, it likely will - based on past experiences. So, we end up with a situation where the value we place on drinking, multiplied by the high likelihood of achieving the desired outcome (relaxation, suppression of negative moods, etc.), equals a strong motivation to continue the habit.

But here's the kicker: what if we started shifting the equation? What if we started questioning the true value of that drink, or the actual likelihood it will deliver the benefits we're seeking? And what if we began identifying and pursuing goals with higher value and likelihood that contribute to our well-being, rather than detract from it? That's where the real magic begins to happen.

Simply put, the strength of your commitment to achieving your goals depends on the value you place on them and the possibility they will be realized. By identifying our motivations for drinking, we can analyze why we drink –perhaps: to get drunk, be more social, escape a problem, manage stress, increase confidence, relax, have fun, or as part of a ritual. Let's first break these down into two overarching categories of motivation –the personal effect motive and the social effect motive. These are broad categories that can overlap. However, they help us define and identify our reasons for drinking. I want to extend to you my profound congratulations for breaking the mold to become the greatest version of yourself. To recognize when something, even in small doses, isn't right. The good news, it's all doable! You can reframe your thinking and habits to form new ones around alcohol.

Personal Effect Motives: The Personal Effect Motives category refers to drinking as a method to cope: the use of alcohol to escape or manage difficult emotions, social settings, and motives. The Social Effect Motive refers to drinking as a social reinforcement and to add elements of celebration at a good time with others. Social effect motives may be inconsequential, but we often mask personal effect motives inside of social effect motives. We may socialize as an excuse or reason to drink to escape or relieve stress. When I was young, I explained my drinking as wanting to have a good time. The reality was that I wanted to alleviate anxiety and feelings of inadequacy to cope.

It Tastes Good: Many people cite the taste as why they crave a nice cold beer or cocktail because ethanol taste unpleasant. Some studies indicate there's more than the taste that may be playing a trick neurologically, making you believe that the taste is what you crave. Ethanol is created from sugars. People predict that sugar preference can make them more prone to crave a drink as it activates some areas of the brain. A study suggests the taste of alcohol may interact with opioid receptors in the brain that mediate how much we like alcohol and perceive the taste as pleasant to get a buzz. Alcohol affects dopamine, a neurotransmitter, and the brain's pleasure center. This dopamine release can cause you to crave a drink and want more. You might want a second, third, or sixth after your first to escape problems or reduce stress – these are widespread reasons why people drink. Alcohol is an addictive substance for this reason.

Work and Finance: You may have had a hard day or a lot of concerns with work or finance. Maybe your relationships are complicated at the moment. Alcohol certainly can alleviate those feelings and emotions. Unfortunately, these life situations don't change, so what happens is that you hit the pause button for a period. However, you may have to deal with these issues at a lower state the next day.

Alcohol increases the likelihood of anxiety in depressed states and affects things like blood pressure, heart rate, and dopamine depletion, the joy pleasure center. So temporarily, you may feel it relieves stress. The reality is that it may magnify the problem in the long run. Remember that while alcohol may appear to be a quick fix, it ultimately contributes to your stress rather than alleviates it.

Social Ease: Alcohol lowers inhibitions in social settings. This can help loosen you up and be more social. I certainly can attest to alcohol making me more confident and outgoing. On the same note, alcohol lowers inhibitions, which can lead us to say and do things we wouldn't say or do otherwise. Most of us have experienced this to some varying degree. It can also lead to risky behaviors such as driving while drinking. The risk-to-reward benefits suggest more risk than reward in social settings. While I would be more social while drinking, I was less social the day following, even avoiding certain situations or individuals. In that sense, drinking had an anti-social effect on my life. If you do anything with regularity, drinking included, it becomes a ritual. I signaled that it was time to stop work with a drink. Without it, my mind wouldn't rest. Or drinking can be linked to occasions. For others, the ritual is Sunday. Football with pitchers of beer or Sunday brunch should include bottomless mimosas. Like anything you do ritually, it becomes a habit. Some are positive, and others are negative. Time can be a reason to drink as it is always five o'clock somewhere.

Rebellion: Take inventory if drinking is an act of rebellion. This word is humorous to me, but it is worth considering. Some dream, especially teenagers, to be a rebel, to defy the rules, and to show that they are different from others. I relate to this in some small way.

Environment: Your alcohol exposure often depends on your environment and surroundings. For example, if you have a job where alcohol is part of the company culture, it is difficult to avoid. I've worked in places where beer is always on tap in the community kitchen, and happy hour is customary. Conversely, if most people in your work and social networks do not drink, the pressure to drink is significantly reduced. It comes down to the adage you are who you hang out with.

Past Experiences: Past experiences with alcohol can help shape your current value of alcohol. Positive experiences may solidify your value more firmly. My past brings forward feelings of youth, excitement, fun, and adventure around drinking. However, the same can be said for negative past experiences, as they can be a deterrent. You likely may have had a mix of both, so stopping will be more challenging if the focus is on positive experiences. If the focus is on the negative experience, this can have the opposite effect and devalue alcohol in your life. These are the most common reasons we drink as individuals and even as a society. Aside from personal reasons, the marketing machine is in perpetual movement. Commercials, sponsorships, billboards, and ads tell us that drinking is normal. Drinking is the life of the party.

So, in addition to our reasons, we have external influences bombarding us daily. At almost every turn, I invite you to explore these reasons. Many of these applied to me at particular times of my life. You may find this to be true for you. I'd say ritual and environment are the factors that both contributed to my drinking and made it difficult to stop. I am very social, and alcohol in our society is a necessary part of social gatherings. I realize now that the positive outcomes of alcohol use are false narratives. Once you step away and put distance between yourself and your relationship with alcohol, it becomes more evident. For now, you may have a hard time buying that. At this point in this journey, I ask you to be mindful of why you drank and what value you placed on these regions.

Overview:

- Environment plays a role in drinking.
- Anxiety is parallel to understanding drinking habits.
- Examining underlying motivations for drinking creates awareness.
- Use value x likelihood formula for shaping goals and drinking decisions.
- Personal effect and social effect motives are underlying reasons for drinking.
- Personal effect motives include taste, work and finance stress, social ease, rebellion, environment, and past experiences.
- Social effect motives suggest that drinking is a way to socialize and have a good time.
- External influences, such as marketing, promote drinking as normal.
- Mindfulness is an important tool to understand personal reasons for drinking.

Time Reclamation

"Lost time is never found again."

- BENJAMIN FRANKLIN.

As we begin this chapter, I want to discuss achieving more than average. Seeking more does not mean we look down on those operating at average levels. Instead, think of it as you demand more than average for yourself. The only comparisons we should have been those we make of ourselves: where we are now and where we envision ourselves in the future to be the best version of ourselves.

Let me illustrate with an example of my own life. I demanded excellence in my own life. I have always tried to be innovative, efficient, and a big-picture thinker. I read books and tried new things. I put in the work I would model. I looked for examples of success. I approached my fitness in the same way. I worked to find the proper diet and the newest innovations in health. I followed those experts to guide me along my fitness journey. But when it came to social events around alcohol, I was the average person when it came to frequency and quantity. This attitude of, well, if they do it, why can't I? But one day, it clicked. Why did I model myself around those who were examples of greatness in all the other areas of my life? But when it comes to my drinking, I modeled the average drinker. The more I analyzed this, the less it made sense. Then I realized I used the average drinking level as an excuse to drink. I convinced myself there was no reason to change if my drinking was normal. Here's the thing, you're reading this to be above average, so we have to ignore most of the behaviors of others to excel to new levels. When you reframe this, you'll see the average societal behaviors as something you want to go beyond. It doesn't make us any better. It simply means we demand more from ourselves on our path.

Recently, I stayed in an enjoyable resort on the beach in Fort Lauderdale. After fishing on a charter boat, I returned to the hotel at about happy hour. The lobby bar was bustling. On my way to grab one of the hotel bicycles, I passed a group of 50-somethings at the bar, taking a break from a work retreat. I was eager to get some fresh air and went for a long ride along the waterfront to watch the sun go down. I grabbed some famous Cuban food before returning to the hotel and my room. I read for 30 minutes and then planned my next day. I was to check out the following day, so I returned to the lobby. About 75% of the gentlemen, I saw hours earlier hadn't moved. More than half of them didn't look like they could stand up straight. But in our society, this happy hour behavior is considered normal.

All I could think about was how much I would have missed had I been at happy hour and not doing what I had planned. The next day I would have been clouded, with a late start, going through the motions until the afternoon. Because I didn't socialize around alcohol the night before, my morning started at 5:00 AM with a trip to the gym, then reading and writing. I planned a full day's work before lunch. If you expect to excel in all areas of your life, including limiting alcohol, you must rise above average social behaviors. Most people are complacent with being average, or they've been programmed to accept this as normal behavior. If that makes them happy, that's fine. But this is our journey, and we do not intend to settle or make comparisons. I don't think I'm better than those guys at the hotel bar. I have decided it's time to let go of observing others and identifying them as normal.

Your new standard is to be extraordinary. You aren't missing out on anything—quite the contrary. For me, the concept of regaining time was the most motivating. Time is non-refundable. You can never get it back. Not only are you losing time in the hours you drink, but you are also losing all the hours when you need to sleep later, combined with the hours and days it takes to recover to your full potential.

When you decide to drink—you're also consuming valuable time. Let's say you spend two hours daily drinking, whether at a bar with friends or at home alone. That's 14 hours a week, 56 hours a month, and a staggering 672 hours a year. Imagine if you invested that time in learning new skills, fostering relationships, or pursuing your passion projects.

There's a cumulative effect. However, it's not only the time you spend drinking. Alcohol disrupts your sleep patterns and prevents you from entering sleep's deep, restorative stages. When you stop drinking, you'll wake up earlier and feel more refreshed. Instead of losing hours to alcohol-induced drowsiness or insomnia, you'll seize the day and make the most of each moment.

Now let's talk about the hangover. When you're hungover, your body is not only physically depleted, but your mind is foggy, and your emotions are low. This state can last for hours, if not an entire day, rendering you unable to be productive or present in your daily activities. By quitting alcohol, you'll eliminate these wasted days and be better equipped to tackle your responsibilities with energy and clarity.

Even small amounts of alcohol harm sleep quality and your entire next day. To back up how much your next day is affected, let's observe a study by Mahesh M. Thakkar published in The Journal of Alcoholism: Clinical and Experimental Research in 2015. The study found that alcohol consumption can significantly decrease the restorative quality of sleep. Participants who consumed just one drink experienced a reduction in sleep quality of 9.3%. In contrast, moderate (2-3 drinks) alcohol consumption led to a 24% decrease in restorative sleep quality, and higher alcohol intake (4-6) was reduced by 39.2%.

To quantify the time you'll regain by quitting alcohol, consider the average hours lost daily. If you spend two hours drinking, lose two hours due to poor sleep (waking at 7 am instead of 5 am), and spend three hours hungover the next day, that's seven hours lost each day you drink. If you drink three days a week, that's 21 hours a week, 84 hours a month, and a staggering 1,092 hours a year!

Now, let's put that into perspective. If you reclaim those 1,092 hours, you'll gain 45 full days a year. If you're drinking daily, that's 106 days or about 30% of your year lost! Think about what you could accomplish in that time!

Overview:

- Time loss: Hours spent drinking, hours lost to poor sleep, and hours spent hungover all contribute to significant time loss.
- Reclaiming time: Quitting alcohol allows for reclaiming lost time for personal growth, fostering relationships, and pursuing passions.
- Impact on sleep: Alcohol decreases sleep quality, affecting productivity and energy levels the next day.
- Quantifying regained time: Quitting alcohol can result in regaining weeks' worth of time per year for personal development.

Alcohol's Impact

"The greatest wealth is health."

- VIRGIL.

It's essential to unmask the health and mental health risks that can arise from alcohol consumption. By understanding the consequences of alcohol on your body, mind, and emotions, you're empowering yourself to make informed choices that lead you toward a life full of energy, passion, and purpose.

The Silent Threat to Physical Health

For in-between drinkers, it's easy to overlook the potential health risks of alcohol consumption. You may not be drinking excessively or experiencing any outward signs of a problem, but alcohol can still profoundly impact your physical health. The risks associated with alcohol consumption can range from cardiovascular issues and digestive problems to weakened immune systems and an increased likelihood of developing certain types of cancer.

One study published in The Lancet (citation) demonstrated that even moderate alcohol consumption could lead to a heightened risk of health issues such as heart disease and stroke. By stepping back and taking a break from alcohol, you're granting your body the opportunity to heal, recover, and thrive.

The Subtle Consequences on Mental Health

The impact of alcohol on mental health often goes unnoticed among in-between drinkers. You might not realize that alcohol can be a double-edged sword when it comes to your emotional and psychological well-being. While it may temporarily relieve stress, alcohol can exacerbate anxiety and depression in the long run.

Research has shown that alcohol disrupts the delicate balance of neurotransmitters in the brain, leading to mood fluctuations, impaired cognitive function, and an increased risk of mental health issues. A study by the National Institutes of Health (NIH) revealed that individuals who took a break from drinking experienced significant improvements in their mental health and overall life satisfaction. By stepping away from alcohol, you're embarking on a journey toward enhanced emotional stability, self-awareness, and inner peace.

Your Journey Towards a Vibrant Life
We must acknowledge the health and mental health risks associated with alcohol consumption, even for in-between drinkers. By taking a break from alcohol, you're not only safeguarding your physical health and nurturing your emotional and psychological well-being.

Embrace this opportunity to transform your life and step into a world overflowing with energy, passion, and purpose. Remember, the power lies within you, and the time to act is now.

Overview:

- Empower yourself with the knowledge to make informed choices
- Physical health risks: cardiovascular issues, digestive problems, weakened immune systems, increased cancer likelihood
- The Lancet study: moderate alcohol consumption heightens health risks
- Mental health risks: exacerbated anxiety and depression, mood fluctuations, impaired cognitive function
- Safeguard physical health and nurture emotional well-being by stepping away from alcohol
- Embrace the opportunity for transformation and a life full of energy, passion, and Purpose

Alcohol & Stress

"It's not stress that kills us, it is our reaction to it."

- HANS SELYE

It's understandable to want a quick fix for stress, and alcohol might seem like the perfect candidate. A tough day at work, feeling overwhelmed, and all you want to do is relax with a glass of your favorite beverage. It seems like the perfect solution. But, in reality, alcohol is not the solution to stress. It is the cause of more stress.

Initially, alcohol can be calming, making it seem like it relieves stress. But here's the thing: that relaxed feeling is temporary and not the whole story. Your current stresses are only pushed off for you to deal with later while in a low-emotional state. It's important to recognize that alcohol doesn't genuinely address the root causes of your stress; it merely masks them for a short period. Here's how alcohol can make stress worse:

Emotional Roller Coaster: Alcohol impacts your brain's neurotransmitters, which can make your emotions go haywire, leaving you feeling more anxious, irritable, or upset – not exactly stress relief. The temporary calm it provides can quickly give way to heightened negative emotions, making it harder to cope with your stressors effectively.

Cloudy Judgment: When you're under the influence, your decision-making skills take a nosedive. Alcohol impairs your ability to think clearly and logically, which can lead to poor choices that you may later regret. These ill-advised decisions can create additional stress and compound existing problems, making it even harder to manage your stress levels effectively.

The Dependence Trap: If you turn to alcohol for stress relief too often, you might start relying on it a little too much. That can lead to a vicious cycle of needing alcohol to deal with stress, creating more stress in the long run. This unhealthy reliance on alcohol can exacerbate your stress levels, rather than relieve them, and may even contribute to the development of alcohol use disorders.

Health Consequences: Regularly overindulging in alcohol can lead to a whole host of health problems, from liver damage to high blood pressure. And let's be honest – dealing with health issues can be a significant stressor. Moreover, excessive alcohol consumption can disrupt your sleep patterns, leaving you feeling fatigued and less able to cope with the challenges of daily life.

Remember that alcohol is a fair-weather friend. It might seem like a quick fix, but in the end, it only adds to your stress. Instead of turning to alcohol, consider healthier ways to manage stress, such as exercise, meditation, or talking to a friend or mental health professional. By addressing the root causes of your stress and developing healthy coping mechanisms, you'll be better equipped to handle life's challenges without relying on alcohol as a crutch.

Overview:

- Alcohol as stress relief: temporary, deceptive relaxation
- Emotional rollercoasters: increased anxiety, irritability, and upset
- Cloudy judgment: poor decision-making, potential regrets
- Dependence trap: a vicious cycle of relying on alcohol for stress relief
- Health consequences: various health problems, added stress
- Overall: alcohol is not a reasonable solution. It contributes to more stress.

Social Puzzle

*"Whenever you find yourself on the side of the majority, it
is time to pause and reflect."*

- MARK TWAIN.

This chapter will cover some of the social influences we likely will encounter on this journey, how they can affect our thoughts and beliefs, and how to change that narrative internally and externally. The social acceptance of alcohol is so strong that it is inevitable that you will encounter people, even close friends, questioning the reasons why you have decided to make this commitment.

One example of this recently happened to me while meeting with a colleague for a drink. And yes, you can still meet for drinks with friends, even if soda and lime are on the menu. Two men sitting beside us ordered a big decanter of wine which they placed on the bar in front of us. We struck up a conversation about what the decanter does to the wine. My friend asked, "Hey, Mike, do you drink? Oh wait, I forgot you don't drink." It was insignificant that he had forgotten, but his comment produced an odd response. One of the men's eyes got really wide. His entire demeanor changed. That comment meant I wasn't part of his club anymore. He may have thought, "This guy must have a problem."

I have become so confident in my beliefs that his response didn't faze me. While I found this encounter humorous, I found it a little sad. You undoubtedly will encounter a similar situation.

Cognitive Dissonance
Picture two friends, Paul and David, who regularly go out for drinks after work. One day, Paul decides to stop drinking. David, who continues drinking, suddenly feels uneasy about his alcohol consumption. This discomfort arises from the conflict between his beliefs and actions, known as cognitive dissonance. To ease this tension, David might judge Paul's decision to quit drinking as unnecessary or even extreme, thus justifying

his own choice to keep drinking. In this case, judgment alleviates David's discomfort and makes his actions feel more justified.

Projection

Imagine a woman named Emily who loves going out with her friends for cocktails. When she meets Linda, a new coworker who chooses not to drink, Emily labels her as boring, uptight, or self-righteous. However, this judgment is not about Linda; it's about Emily's fears and doubts about her drinking habits. Emily unconsciously projects her insecurities onto Linda to avoid facing her concerns about her lifestyle.

Social Identity Theory

Take the example of Amy, a college student who is an active sorority member, where heavy drinking is the norm. In this close-knit group, alcohol is vital to their social bonding. When Amy encounters Jessica, a fellow student who chooses not to drink, she immediately judges her as unfriendly and rigid. But Amy's judgment is not really about Jessica's character; it's about her need to protect her social identity as a sorority member. By labeling Jessica as an outsider, Amy can reinforce her sense of belonging and maintain the positive image of her social group.

By examining these story-like examples, we can better understand the complex psychological reasons why people who drink might judge those who don't. As we learn to recognize these underlying motives, we can develop greater empathy, self-awareness, and the ability to foster genuine connections with others, regardless of their lifestyle choices.

Overview:

- Social influences on the alcohol journey
- Encountering judgment from others
- Cognitive dissonance: conflicting beliefs and actions
- Projection: judging others to avoid self-reflection
- Social Identity Theory: protecting group belonging
- Develop empathy, self-awareness, and genuine connections

Manifestation Principle

"Your beliefs become your thoughts, your thoughts become your words, your words become your actions, your actions become your habits, your habits become your values, your values become your destiny."

- MAHATMA GANDHI.

The Law of Attraction or Manifestation Principle has gained immense popularity in recent decades. Although its name may be relatively new, the belief system behind it has been around for centuries, if not a millennium. We manifest our reality daily through our minds, thoughts, and intentions.

We generally accept this to be true. For example, if we write down our goals and focus on them daily, our likelihood of achieving them increases. The same applies to our thoughts and beliefs. Whether we label it as God, source, energy, or the universe, what we send out comes back to us. Have you ever thought about someone you haven't heard from in a while, only to receive a call or text from that person shortly after? This experience isn't a coincidence and happens frequently. It isn't limited to people we'd like to hear from. The same occurs when we focus on someone we don't want to hear from.

I used to be skeptical about sending thoughts out and having them return in a seemingly magical way If you think this is too woo-woo, I understand. But after decades of experiencing and observing this phenomenon, I have no doubt there's truth to it.

In this chapter, let's understand that the Law of Attraction doesn't differentiate between desired and undesired. It applies equally to positive and negative thoughts. Regarding drinking and alcohol, we need to examine our thoughts and beliefs to align them with our intentions, making the change process more manageable.

Drinking can stir up many unhappy emotions and thoughts, hijacking our focus. We need to break this vicious cycle to achieve the change we desire. The constant self-attacks we inflict upon ourselves directly correlate to what we attract into our lives. If we think we have no self-control and don't deserve what we have, we attract more of the same – less self-control.

Drinking can lower our self-worth and increase depression and anxiety, exacerbating our negative self-talk. Recognizing and reframing that these thoughts and beliefs attract the desired outcomes is crucial. Consider the following examples of negative and positive inner dialogues:

Negative: "I can't seem to stop. It's impossible. I'm weak. I make these stupid decisions, just like typical me. It is what it is. It's what I deserve. I'm not going to drink tonight, but we'll see. I'll probably fail again."

Positive: "You know what? I made a mistake, but that doesn't define who I am. I am strong and worthy of happiness. I can do this. By skipping the drinks tonight, I give gratitude for waking up tomorrow refreshed, recharged, happy, and ready to achieve all my goals. It's my intention today to accept this gift."

Which one of these inner dialogues is more likely to lead to success? We aren't talking about just self-talk. There's more at play here. We are sending a signal into the ether, a signal that somehow returns to us and manifests in our lives. Instead of focusing on the negative, we must concentrate on the positive and the benefits we deserve.

Mental imagery conditions the brain for successful outcomes. Athletes who use visualization know the power of positive thinking. When they visualize successful competitions, they stimulate the same brain regions as when they physically perform the same action.

The key is how we frame our intended future actions. The mind and the universe don't interpret "don't" or "won't." What we concentrate on is what we attract in our life. If we constantly tell ourselves, "I won't drink tonight," that becomes our focus and it's accepted as "I will drink tonight." We need to reframe the narrative. Instead of being negative and restrictive, we need to flip the narrative to positivity and abundance. For example:

"I will make a healthy decision for myself tonight. I look forward to waking up early, bright-eyed, and rested. I intend to live a healthy lifestyle and accept all the incredible benefits of those decisions."

Reframing the narrative shifts the focus from what you wish to avoid to what you intend to manifest in your life. By cultivating positive thoughts and embracing the abundance of a healthy lifestyle, you're better equipped to make lasting changes and create the reality you truly desire.

Now let's shift to the concept of self-sabotage. Self-sabotage occurs more often than we realize in various aspects of our lives. It's something we all do, consciously or subconsciously, that prevents us from achieving a goal, milestone, or accomplishment. To illustrate this concept, let's consider an individual in a relationship who does not feel they deserve love, fearing rejection. Consequently, they might cheat on their spouse with the mindset, "I'll hurt you before you hurt me."

This person has created self-sabotaging behaviors, even though external factors had nothing to do with their actions. Self-sabotaging behaviors with alcohol often emerge close to a milestone. As we examine our behaviors, it's crucial to note setting goals of 30, 60, 90 days, or one year is common. The pattern is that we make self-sabotaging decisions just short of those milestones. So, we must ask ourselves, why is that?

These behaviors generally stem from two distinct sources, the first is rooted in self-worth, and the second is grounded in fear of significant change. As new goals and changes begin to unfold, especially when we are close to reaching these goals, the idea of "I am not worthy" obstructs progress. We stop what we perceive as something we aren't worthy of. You are outside your comfort zone when you make substantial changes in your life and trigger responses like:

- Fear of judgment: I don't want to explain myself to friends.
- Fear of the unknown: How will I handle stress now that everything is different?
- Fear of failure: I'm never going to make it. I should give up now.
- Fear of loss: I'll never get to party or sit on a beach with a drink.

The list can be long and personal. If we experience self-sabotaging behaviors, we must first observe if and when they appear. This observation is crucial to recognizing thought patterns and discounting their validity. The mind has significant power to convince us that thoughts working against us are good for us. If we learn to observe and control these moments, it gives us power. Feelings of power lead to confidence in our resolve to trust the process and the journey we have committed to. We can confidently and openly welcome and embrace significant change without fear, stepping out of our comfort zone.

In the following section, we'll discuss action steps for using the law of attraction. The first step is to think positively. It may sound cliché, but it's vital. It's normal for us to focus on what we want to avoid rather than what we want to attract. Let go of those avoidance ideas, as they don't serve you and are exhausting. Positivity will energize you and attract precisely that. So, we need to raise our energy, frequency, and positive outcomes we want to attract by being caring, loving, joyful, and grateful for the life we live and the one we intend to manifest. Understanding this concept is the first step we can take. However, it requires action to put it to work in our lives. The best way to do this is with journaling. If you don't currently journal, it's not as difficult as you think. I was never one to journal until around 40. Now it's become a habit every morning like clockwork, my pen to paper is there waiting. Not only is it a small task, but it's also one of the most important steps for self-development. There is no strict formula to adhere to; this is your journal and your thoughts.

Let's cover some guidelines to help you get started or, if you already journal, incorporate them into your process. Affirmations are positive and written in the present tense. They can be statements about things in your life or something you want to attract. When we write in the present tense about something we want, we envision it already being there. This invokes the emotions surrounding the desire. Imagine how it will feel, placing yourself in a positive mental state to achieve it.

For example, "I am happily living without alcohol. Every morning, I wake up full of love, gratitude, and energy for the day. I can reach my goals more easily with this new focus. I'm living the life I'm meant to and looking forward to all the great things ahead. I am happy and loved." Take the initiative to create affirmations that reflect who you want to become and how it makes you feel. By doing this, you bridge the mental gap between the present and the future –what you want to experience by envisioning it. Experiencing the positive emotions surrounding our affirmation encourages and motivates us to take action to close the gap between where we are now and where we want to be.

Understanding our current state and goals is essential as we move forward. For some, your goal is complete abstinence from alcohol beyond our 66-day commitment. For others, your goal may be to reset your current relationship with alcohol to a healthier level. It's also okay if you're unsure; this is entirely normal. As we head into uncharted territories, there are two significant commitments we must lay the foundation for moving forward. The first is the obvious—your commitment to this program. The second is our long-term goal after completing this program. It's hard to predict the future in the face of massive change.

I can guarantee your goals will be questioned or changed along the way. This fluidity is to be expected and entirely acceptable. I intend to arm you with the knowledge to make those decisions today or along the journey. The specific timing of the decision doesn't matter as long as we make them between now and the end of the 66 days.

Overview:

- The Law of Attraction has ancient roots and manifests reality through thoughts and intentions.
- It applies to both positive and negative thoughts.
- Drinking can stir up negative emotions and thoughts, hijacking focus.
- To attract desired outcomes, reframe negative self-talk into positive.
- Mental imagery conditions the brain for success, as seen in athletes' visualization practices
- Focus on positive intentions instead of avoidance
- Self-sabotage can hinder progress, often rooted in self-worth or fear of significant changes
- Raise energy and frequency through positive thoughts and emotions
- Journaling can help apply The Law of Attraction in daily life
- Use affirmations in the present tense to envision a desired reality

Journal Power

"In the journal, I do not just express myself more openly than I could to any person; I create myself."

- SUSAN SONTAG.

We've now reached the most actionable sections of this book. I've laid a solid foundation for reshaping our relationship with alcohol by examining how we should perceive it, how it has influenced our life, and the life we aspire to build. Relying solely on willpower is neither a strategy nor sufficient to modify our habits. If it were, you wouldn't be reading this book. Instead, you'd wake up one day and stop.

Lasting change crumbles in the absence of a dependable framework. This section provides a framework to initiate and maintain your dedication to cultivating new habits.

The Power of Journaling

From my personal experience, I want to emphasize the power of journaling to create change and contribute to overall happiness and well-being. If you aren't someone who is the journaling type, that's okay. Only in the last few years have I made it a practice. Not only has it become something I practice, but also it has become a ritual. The effects are so noticeable that I don't leave town on business trips or vacations without my journal. My journal comes with me. Journaling allows you to focus on the positives in your life, offer gratitude, and document your efforts toward your goals. Our minds operate at an incredible rate. If you remember from a previous chapter, approximately 60,000 thoughts per day.

Focusing on our gratitude and goals is extremely difficult with all that mental activity. You may think that journaling involves writing a "dear diary" account of your entire day, or an inner monologue. While that is a form of journaling, it is not how we will use this powerful tool. Instead, we will focus on simple observations and give gratitude for what we have envisioned for ourselves. The point of journaling is to provide direction for our lives. By journaling, we are grateful that we uncover the steps we must take to reach our goals.

This book has a journaling framework you can follow. But, by all means, expand on it! The only rule is to be positive and constructive. Reframe your thoughts as opportunities for learning and growth. Feel free to indulge if you encounter difficult moments as long as you're not having a pity party or being pessimistic.

To give you an example of why journaling is important, let me share the results of a study. Participants agreed to a small biopsy that created a lesion on the arm. Researchers asked the participants to journal within specific guidelines. And they asked half of the participants to share their thoughts and feelings. The other half were told to write about time management. The participants journaled for 20 minutes over three days. By day 11, 76% of the group who wrote openly about their feelings had fully healed. By contrast, only 42% of those who wrote about time management had recovered. Significantly, we have proof that journaling affects our mental well-being, improves our physical well-being, and dramatically affects our outcomes.

The first step is to recognize the power of journaling to change our lives, making it both essential and fun. Journal with whatever means you have at hand. Find a journal dedicated to your mindful practice or go to a store of your liking or a stationary specialty store. Find a pen that you enjoy writing with. I like a brown leather journal with an elastic strap that keeps the book closed with my pen neatly inside. I love a good gliding gel pen in black ink. These are just examples. Find what speaks to you. You might prefer a brightly colored book and various colored inks. It doesn't matter. What matters is making the experience something uniquely you. Next, I want you to write an intention on the opening page of your journal for three days. Writing your goals increases your success rate.

I share my morning intention as one example: "I wake up full of life, love, and energy every morning. I am living my life's purpose to my full potential. I easily accomplish my goals personally and professionally with my newfound passion for life." All this carries over to creating and maintaining an inspiring home where Priscilla, the kids, and I can love and live our dream life.

Make sure to write these goals as if they have already happened, even if they have not. In your own way, I invite you to explore your intentions. Your images can be of a family and loved ones or maybe a beach that's a dream paradise. Feel free to use my images as well. The power of words combined with images is a combo for experiencing gratitude, love, and achieving your goals.

Review Your Statement of Purpose

As we discussed previously, your statement of purpose is one of the anchoring techniques to remind you why and where you are going. By reading it, or even better, saying it aloud, you send a message to your subconscious of what you intend to achieve and what you are worthy to receive to the law of attraction. It will come to you with repetition and true belief in your power to receive. For those of you on the fence about this, that's understandable. It's an act of faith. But I promise you, with practice, it will stick with you. It will make you a believer. If you wholeheartedly move forward with your statement, you will manifest it as your reality. Recite your statement in the morning before journaling and once before bed. Read it out loud with belief. Hold it in your heart to be true.

When To Journal

Journal every day. Timing is a personal preference. I prefer to journal in the early morning with a fresh and clear mind, which allows me to plant the seeds for what the day will yield. I start my day by being grateful for what I have and intend to manifest. Doing this ritual in the evening is also of great benefit. It can free your mind as a reminder after a long day.

For some, journaling freezes your day's thoughts and sets intentions before bed. Journaling can also replace the witching hour habit when you may be tempted to reach for a drink. There is no specific time you must journal as long as you do. However, I urge you to consider journaling in the early mornings -- it allows you to have gratitude for your newfound clarity during the hour you gained that you would have lost sleeping or when in a frantic rush out the door. The early mornings also provide much more consistency. The middle of the day or the evenings tend to have more variation and distraction. It's also easier to put things off or forget in the evenings. So, while I don't put a hard rule on any of this, I suggest the early morning as an enjoyable daily ritual.

The Cumulative Effect

As the saying goes, Rome wasn't built in a day but day by day, brick by brick. With intention, we form our habits. Every journal entry is an extra brick laid in the building of our foundation. Then from the foundation, we continue to build an impeccable fortress. Writing in our daily journal allows us to build on the previous days, weeks, and months. It allows us to see this journey as it unfolds. As you move forward, aside from the changes you witness every day, you'll have a record of your transformation. Your journal allows you to reflect on and recognize the stages of transformation you are experiencing. As humans, we have short memories at times. It's easy to focus on our problems today and forget how far we have come, even in a short period. There's something deeply gratifying when you complete an entire journal with your thoughts, setbacks, and wins. Your journal is the tool that allows you to review and reflect and to anchor further your commitment to meaningful and lasting improvement in love and harmony, confidence and release, and self-acceptance.

The Science of the Pen-to-Paper

Behavioral Neuroscience is a journal that publishes research articles on neural bases of behavior. They recently cited a study that tracked students taking notes by hand versus those taking notes on a digital device. They found that those writing by hand exhibited increased brain activity in areas associated with language imagery, and visualization in the hippocampus, the part of the brain responsible for memory and neuro opening. The study suggests the neurological benefits of handwriting notes, essays, or journal entries by hand that are not achieved using digital devices. Note-taking by hand activates the mind's eye to recall what has been written, creating a connection to the words and thoughts behind them. This allows the brain to follow and focus in a way that supports understanding and learning. My anecdotal experience supports this claim. When my pen hits the paper, I can let the world in, and my words flow, free to cross out or underline, write in the margins, draw, or sketch. This entire book is written freehand in notebooks. I'm free to revisit, read, or revise any part of the writing.

Also, handwriting my thoughts keeps me focused since I'm easily distracted. Research verifies that pen-to-paper note-taking expands memory, recall, creativity, and visualization ability. In summary, old-school writing is the preferred method for journaling our intentions for achieving our desires.

Overview:

- Techniques are outlined to initiate and maintain a dedication to new habits, emphasizing the power of journaling.
- Journaling benefits our mental and physical well-being.
- A suggested journaling framework: be positive and constructive and write intentions and goals as if they are achieved.
- Review your statement of purpose: recite each morning and evening to reinforce intentions.
- Journal daily, timing is a personal preference, but early morning or evening is recommended.
- The cumulative effect of journaling: builds a foundation, tracks your transformation, allows reflection, and anchors your commitment to improvement.
- Science of pen to paper: Handwriting notes enhances brain activity; therefore, the pen-to-paper method is preferred for journaling.

PART

04

Tools & Techniques

"Take the first step in faith. You don't have to see the whole staircase, just take the first step."

- MARTIN LUTHER KING JR.

Start Day

When is the perfect day to start? Not to burst your bubble, but there will never be a perfect day to start any challenge. That said, there are steps that we can take to better our start. Find a day free of any changes in your schedule. If you're getting ready to go on a work trip or vacation in the next week, then have a good time. Be mindful of your drinking, but don't think you must commit to this occasion. You will quickly see how much you gain from giving up drinking. However, this insight happens more frequently the more distance you put between yourself and old habits. Beyond the obvious of making, it difficult, we don't want you to associate your commitment with sacrifice, far from it. For now, we will forego situations with perceived sacrifice. So, if we are on a week away from a major holiday, a ballgame, a work function, et cetera, let's allow ourselves to remove the pressure of those potentially tricky situations.

Additionally, think about your regular habits. What days do you typically indulge the most? The weekends are calm, so stopping on a Friday might not be the best choice if that's the case. Alternatively, maybe there's a situation where drinking isn't possible, which might make for a great start date. We are looking for a date not more than three weeks from now and a situation that presents no significant challenges or high stress.

It also doesn't have to be overly complicated. Your life is happening as we look for the path of least resistance. There will always be travel celebrations, happy hour, and more. We can count on it. There will never be a perfect day to stop. Instead, I firmly believe sooner rather than later -- if today is the day, amazing. If it is ten days from now, equally amazing. It's essential you choose a date to increase your probability of success rather than to procrastinate. Be mindful. If you have a life partner or significant other, read on. If not, you can skip this short section. Getting your partner in sync with your new journey is important for several reasons. Generally, you will be in one of two situations, one that your partner is entirely on board, maybe asking for this change as well. The other is indifference or even resistance. In either case, you need to have a conversation to emphasize precisely why you have dedicated yourself to this path.

Review the goals together so your partner can understand why you are committed to abstaining from alcohol. Ask for their support and warn them that this journey is difficult. They need to be excited about what is the come. They also need to understand the reason for the 66-day requirement and how their response will either help or hinder your path.

Your partner can be a cheerleader urging you on, or they can be a crutch for making excuses. In my case, we had to discuss its importance for us as partners. Luckily, I had a fully supportive partner. I needed her to help me stay strong. At the same time, she didn't see the same problems that I was feeling due to abstaining from alcohol. So, in moments of trial and error, she would do what she felt was most supportive. She would tell me not to be so hard on myself or feel guilty if I broke my commitment. Her response was her kind side, and I appreciated her kindness. Over time, I realized I needed a different kind of kindness that helped me stick to my resolve with less empathy for mistakes.

I didn't ask her to tell me no or to guilt me. These decisions are ultimately mine. I did not want a babysitter. I asked her to remind me of my goals and intentions, which changed her level of support. Unless your partner volunteers to take a break from alcohol alongside you, I'd advise you not to ask this of them, as it is a personal choice. If you are in a situation where your partner should also abstain, the best way to encourage that path is by example. They may not be ready today. What could be pivotal to their decision is for you to show the benefits of taking a break from alcohol. Truthfully answering their questions helps solidify the working relationship. Make it clear that this is your choice and that you aren't asking them to do the same.

There are things your partner can do to support you. The first is to limit your access to alcohol. We never had a stocked reserve in our home, mostly because I enjoyed the ritual of going to the store and choosing what I would drink that night. I also worried about an unlimited supply in my home. If alcohol is always in your home, it might be a good idea to place it in an out-of-the-way location. When my wife would buy wine or stock up for an upcoming party, she would be mindful of putting it in the back of the pantry instead of on the counter or in plain sight. I didn't want to say or ask, let's not have alcohol in the house. She was motivated to do this because she knew abstaining was important to me. She made alcohol inconspicuous in our home. She understood my commitment, and in doing so, she took steps to support this commitment. You will have instances when your partner or other family members help or hinder your journey. That is why I don't list do's and don'ts. The answer to the best support will naturally unfold in your home. If you are in sync with your partner, they will naturally take steps to support your journal journey.

You won't be the only one making big changes, so reviewing the goals together is essential. This is especially true in the first week or two, depending on your level of drinking. You may experience irritability, restlessness, or insomnia, leading to other difficulties. For me, it was all of these. Priscilla knew that might be coming. She also gave me some extra understanding and grace to get through those times. Fortunately, these challenges are usually very short-lived. Your partner can remind you of your reasons for taking a break. "It's okay if you might not be yourself right now, but I know you are doing this to be a better person, a better partner, healthier, and more present for the family." You want and need to communicate with your ally on this journey as one of the keys to success.

Declaration of Intention

We talked about writing a statement of purpose. The statement of purpose is the life you intend to manifest through your new commitment. The declaration of intention will define what we are prepared to do in order to achieve our purpose.

We create clarity and increase our success rate by writing our declaration of intention – a simple and quick exercise that will significantly impact our success. For example, "I declare to make a healthy change to achieve more [benefit 1, benefit 2, benefit 3]. Starting on [day/month/year] and for the next 66 days, I will take all the necessary steps to realize this declaration. I'm 100% committed to achieving my goals." With this statement, we are doing three critical things to anchor your commitment. The first is anchoring a date associated with the change to build upon that date moving forward. The second is reframing the statement to include positive affirmations rather than negations focusing on sacrifice, such as stating you are "stopping" or "giving up." These words don't serve us. You have much more to gain than give up.

So, we will focus on what you gain with these three aspects you hope to improve in your life. Finally, we declare a specific time, affirm we are prepared to take action, and have nothing less than a 100% commitment to these goals and your declaration. I call this declaration our time to plant our flag in the sand. It's our moment to burn the ships and give no option to turn them back. Take this declaration and attach it to your statement or purpose. One of the things I do to remind myself of my declaration is to simply put my commitment date on the front of the refrigerator. That way, I'm constantly reminded of my commitment throughout the day and evening. The day you accomplish your goals is a day of celebration. On this day, you should verbally acknowledge that you have embraced more of what you hope to gain in your life -- a happier, healthier, more fulfilling life for you and a day to celebrate more love and appreciation for those around you. Make your declaration and keep it close.

Overview:

- There is no perfect day to begin a challenge.
- Choose a low-stress day: avoid major holidays, events, or disruptions in schedule.
- Consider your habits: choose a start date that avoids days of indulgence or high stress.
- Include your partner: communicate goals and intentions; seek support and understanding.
- Limit access to alcohol: make it less visible and accessible at home.
- Understand temporary challenges: irritability, restlessness, and insomnia may occur in the early stages.
- Write a statement of purpose: declare your intentions, set a date, and commit 100% to your goals.
- Focus on gains: emphasize improvements in your life rather than your sacrifices.
- Keep your declaration visible: display your commitment date as a constant reminder.
- Celebrate successes: acknowledge your progress and personal growth.

Slipping Up

"You are allowed to be both a masterpiece and a work in progress, simultaneously."

- SOPHIA BUSH.

As we continue our journey to change habits around alcohol, you might be as we continue our journey to change habits around alcohol, you might be wondering what happens if you slip up. Do you start over on day one? The answer to this is: it depends on the extent of the slip-up and how far into the 66 days you are. In this chapter, we'll establish guidelines to help you decide how to proceed if a slip-up occurs and explore how to maintain motivation and commitment.

Research suggests that habit change is a gradual process, and breaking from a commitment for one day does not necessarily disrupt the formation of new habits. Habits are built through consistent repetition and reinforcement over time. While a temporary lapse in commitment may slow down progress, it doesn't erase the progress made up to that point. Instead, it's important to acknowledge setbacks as part of the journey and continue working towards the desired change in habits. Consistency and persistence in practicing new behaviors are key factors in successfully forming new habits.

Remember, setbacks are a natural part of the process, and how you handle them can make a significant difference in your overall success. Nothing erases the previous days of commitment, regardless of the number. The goal here is not to give you a cop-out but to offer grace and understanding as you work toward lasting change.

Guideline 1: The 14-Day Rule
If the slip-up happens within the first 14 days, start back at day one. The first 14 days are crucial for reducing cravings, so getting through this period without drinking is essential to building a solid foundation.

Guideline 2: One-Time Forgiveness

More than one slip-up in 66 days means starting back at day one. There is no allowable cheat day. If the slip-up is unplanned, spend the next day observing what made you have a momentary break from your commitment to 66 days without drinking. Be 100% honest with yourself. If you feel you cheated and will feel unfulfilled in 65 out of 66 days, start at day one. However, if starting back at day one means you give in, then make whatever decision leads to continuing not to drink and improving your habits, health, and mental well-being.

Guideline 3: Consider the Depth of Your Habits

The heavier or more frequent your drinking was, the stricter you should be in considering restarting on day one. Evaluate the depth of your habits and honestly assess how best to proceed.

Guideline 4: Excessive Binge Drinking

Suppose your slip-up involves excessive binge drinking, reset to day one. The misstep indicates a need to address the underlying issues that led to the relapse.

In these guidelines, you must evaluate what happened and what feels right for you. Even if that means starting over from day one after day 51, nothing will erase the previous days of commitment. Adding another 66 days on top of that will only further anchor your new habits.

You are responsible for your success. The only cheating will be you cheating yourself. The key to navigating slip-ups is to learn from your mistakes, allow grace for yourself in the process, and stay committed to change. In the next chapter, we'll explore additional strategies and tools to help you overcome challenges, develop a healthier relationship with alcohol, and maintain your progress beyond the 66-day commitment.

Overview:

- Setbacks are natural: Understand setbacks are part of the process; learn from them.
- Breaking from a commitment for one day does not necessarily disrupt the formation of new habits
- Guideline 1: 14-Day Rule: Restart at day one if a slip-up occurs within the first 14 days.
- Guideline 2: One-Time Forgiveness: More than one slip-up in 66 days means starting over.
- Guideline 3: Assess Habit Depth: Heavier or more frequent drinking requires stricter restarting
- Guideline 4: Binge Drinking: Reset to day one if a slip-up involves excessive binge drinking
- Evaluate and learn: Determine the best course of action based on your situation and feelings.
- Stay committed: Focus on learning from mistakes, allowing grace, and continuing to change.

Support Network

*"Accountability is the glue that ties commitment
to results."*

- BOB PROCTOR.

I cannot overstate the value of having an accountability partner. It's essential to surround yourself with supportive individuals who understand and champion your goals. Accountability partners do more than just check in; they are a pillar of encouragement, motivation, and reassurance. They witness your highs, lows, and every pivotal moment in between.

Accountability is a simple relationship where you ask someone you trust if they will hold you accountable for your commitment and goals. You explain that you are reading a book that lays out a plan to help you take a break from alcohol. Based on scientific research, the book maintains it takes 66 days to reset and change habits.

Here are some templates to initiate the dialogue. The aim is to spark interest without overwhelming them with details. Once they express interest, you can provide more guidance on what would make the accountability partnership most beneficial for you.

Template 1:
Hey [Friend's Name],

I'm setting out on a 66-day journey to reset my habits with alcohol. The book says having a solid friend like you could make a huge difference. Would you consider being my go-to for occasional check-ins and real talk? I would appreciate it greatly!

Take care,
[Your Name]

Template 2:
Hey [Friend's Name],

I'm kicking off a 66-day challenge to shift my habits around alcohol. It's a big commitment and having a trusted friend for support would mean the world. Are you open to being my accountability partner? I'm looking for someone to share updates with and maybe celebrate milestones here and there.

Thanks,
[Your Name]

The response to this request is often one of support and admiration. It is that simple. I've never experienced or heard of a negative response.

Approaching someone this way can feel humbling or seem like an admission of weakness. I know from experience. But we need the insight to reinterpret this. This approach demonstrates pure courage and strength. A typical response is, "That's amazing. I'm excited for you. How can I help?" You clarify what support looks like when you struggle to keep the course and ask them to note any positive changes along the way.

The most significant impact on me in having someone hold me accountable wasn't always the ongoing support. It was having the initial conversation. The effort and commitment I had to make internally to have the conversation strengthened my resolve. Your partner is a great source of support. I'm asking you to take it further and consider who else you can recruit for your team. Who can you be open with and trust will support this journey? You will be surprised at how excited and happy you are when you find the right person. I can almost guarantee this also will be your experience in self-accountability.

As you move forward, your accountability strengthens over time with our commitment. There's one thing I can promise: you will witness drastic improvements in your life. I want you to write a list of your progress over time. It's common to take improvements for granted, not just in this situation but in many other areas of life. For example, when I bought my new truck, that was my baby. I was sure to protect that new interior from my wild young kids, but I watched it less over time. The truck became something I owned. It wasn't fresh or new to me. This also happens in other areas of our lives. First, we take notes and celebrate the change, but it soon becomes the new normal. When this happens, we may no longer value the change the same way we celebrated it before. So, take special attention to noting these changes as a tool for our accountability. Here are some steps to follow:

Step 1: Choose the Right Accountability Partner

Family / Friend: Selecting the right accountability partner is crucial. It may not be easy to ask for help, but it's essential to understand that people are often more than willing to lend a hand. Avoid choosing a partner who has a strong opinion about alcohol, as their philosophy might not align with the methods we are using. While these individuals can be wonderful people with a wealth of knowledge, such programs have a very strict belief system that differs from the principles of this book. Instead, opt for someone who doesn't drink or drinks only occasionally and would be supportive of your change. This approach will ensure that your accountability partner is better aligned with your objectives and will be more effective in helping you achieve your goals.

- Shares or understands your goal.
- Communicates effectively and regularly.
- Offers positive reinforcement.
- Avoids negativity or judgment.
- Is reliable and consistent.
- Aligns with the principles and approach you're following.

Virtual Assistant: If you're hesitant to involve a friend or peer for accountability, an alternative that may be more comfortable for you is to hire a virtual or personal assistant. Many companies offer personal assistant services at affordable rates, typically ranging from $3 to $5 per hour. This way, you can hire them to check in on you daily or multiple times, depending on your preference.

For example, a virtual assistant could send you a message every morning, asking how you're feeling, how your day is going, and whether you're facing any challenges. They could also text or email you in the evening, asking if you've successfully navigated your day without alcohol and offering support if needed.

Some popular platforms where you can find virtual assistants include Upwork and Freelancer.

These platforms offer a wide range of professional assistants to find someone who matches your needs and communication style. Hiring a virtual assistant can provide a discreet and supportive environment for you to be honest and open about your journey to take a break from alcohol.

When choosing a virtual assistant, review their profiles, read customer reviews, and even conduct a brief interview to ensure they will fit your specific needs well. With the right assistant, you can have a non-judgmental and reliable source of support as you navigate this period of change in your life.

- Explore platforms like Upwork and Freelancer.
- Set a budget for hiring.
- Check reviews and testimonials.
- Conduct preliminary interviews to gauge compatibility.

Step 2: Initiate the Conversation
The most significant step in building your accountability relationship is the first conversation. Be open about your goal to take a 66-day break from alcohol and ask if they are willing to hold you accountable. Remember, this act of vulnerability demonstrates courage and strength. Most people will be supportive and admire your decision.

- Approach the potential partner and share your goal.
- Explain why you're seeking an accountability partner.
- Express how important their support would be to you.

Step 3: Define the Support

Clarify what support looks like for you during this journey. Let your partner know how they can help you stay on track, and ask them to note any positive changes. The initial conversation will likely strengthen your resolve and commitment to your goal.

- Discuss and agree upon communication frequency (e.g., daily, weekly).
- Share preferred methods of communication (e.g., text, call, email)
- Clarify what support you seek (e.g., daily check-ins, reminders, encouragement).
- Set boundaries or topics to avoid.

Step 4: Build Your Support Network

While your partner is an excellent source of support, don't hesitate to recruit more people to your team. Consider who else you can trust and who will be excited to support you on this journey. You'll be pleasantly surprised by how happy and fulfilled you'll feel when you find the right person.

Step 5: Maintain Accountability and Track Progress

As you progress, your accountability will strengthen with your commitment. Remember to write a list of your improvements and achievements over time. We commonly take these changes for granted, but acknowledging them will help maintain your accountability.

- Decide on a regular check-in schedule.
- Set milestones or mini goals along the way.
- Celebrate successes, no matter how small.
- Reflect on challenges and strategize solutions together.

Step 6: Focus on Self-Accountability and Positive Reinforcement

Emphasize positive reinforcement rather than negative. If you start questioning your commitment, remind yourself of the positive changes in your life. Remember that all actions have consequences; breaking your commitment means losing what you've gained. Hold yourself accountable for the consequences of your actions.

- Schedule periodic reviews of the partnership.
- Discuss what's working and what could be improved.
- Adjust communication or support methods as needed.

Building a solid support network and maintaining accountability with a partner and yourself will help you succeed in your 66-day break from alcohol. You'll witness significant improvements in your life by choosing the right partner, initiating the conversation, defining the support, building a network, maintaining accountability, and focusing on positive reinforcement.

Overview:

- Accountability forms: the self and others
- Choose the right partner: Peer, friend, family, or virtual assistant
- Initiate the conversation: Share goals, request support
- Define support: Clarify expectations, positive observations
- Build a support network: Recruit additional trusted individuals
- Maintain accountability: Track progress, improvements
- Focus on self-accountability: Positive reinforcement, consequences awareness
- Achieve the goal: the 66-day break from alcohol with strong support and accountability

The Journal Framework

"Journaling is like whispering to one's self and listening at the same time."

MINA MURRAY.

I will lay out for you the general reasons for our framework. First, however, I want to remind you that journaling is for you. You aren't journaling for anyone else to read. There are no formal rules. Write about what feels right. Grammar and words, who cares? Let your mind flow freely through your hand--if it's three pages, one day, and three sentences, another, great. As long as you journal with your incredible uniqueness and intention to change, you are on the right path to greatness.

Gratitude

Always start your journal with gratitude. This single practice alone will significantly affect all areas of your life. Daily gratitude produces increased positivity, happiness, and self-esteem, reduces stress, and improves health. It's human to set to get caught up in the daily grind and take all the beautiful things that already exist in our lives for granted. Take time to write your appreciation for them. Some examples are gratitude for your kids and partner, your health, sobriety, spirituality, and a warm bed. It doesn't always have to be big things. It can be for the random kindness of someone at the grocery store that reminds you of how wonderful people are. I focus on a few big ones and a small one every day.

Recent Wins

Acknowledging even our small wins encourages us and boosts our confidence. We naturally concentrate on all we need to do and achieve while overlooking all we have done. So, after giving gratitude, we should also recognize our wins. Wins come in all sizes and forms. They don't have to be pivotal. They can be as simple as ensuring you are at home for dinner or taking time with your son or daughter at the park. Maybe it's even showing a level head in a difficult situation where you may have normally lost composure. The incredible thing is you don't have to look for these wins. With all the added time and mental well-being, you will find wins like this flow freely toward you daily.

There is a quote that has always resonated with me. So, let's take the time daily to celebrate these wins. Give praise where praises are due. This daily feed will give your perspective about your to-do list and goals and contribute to the cumulative effect. You improve and accomplish your goals increasingly day by day. Your daily decisions create your destiny.

As we venture deeper into this chapter, we'll be diving into three powerful concepts that lay the foundation for changing our relationship with alcohol: Motivational Enhancement Therapy (MET), Cognitive-Behavioral Therapy (CBT), and Habit Reversal Training (HRT). Now, I've woven these techniques throughout the book without explicitly labeling them, but it's crucial for you to recognize their presence as you engage in the journaling exercises. Before we explore each concept in our practice of journaling, let's take a moment to clarify what they are:

Motivational Enhancement Therapy (MET) is an approach that focuses on you and your intrinsic motivation to change. By helping you explore and resolve any conflicting feelings, MET strengthens your personal commitment to change, sets achievable goals, and develops a plan to reach those goals. This method will empower you to take charge of your journey and fuel your desire for lasting transformation.

Cognitive-Behavioral Therapy (CBT) is a therapeutic technique that sheds light on the connection between your thoughts, feelings, and behaviors. By pinpointing and challenging unhelpful thought patterns, CBT allows you to replace them with healthier, more constructive alternatives. This strategy will be instrumental in helping you overcome self-defeating beliefs and make better choices in your relationship with alcohol.

Habit Reversal Training (HRT) is a practical approach that helps you identify triggers and replace unwanted habits with more desirable ones. By understanding the cues that lead to undesired behaviors, HRT equips you with the tools to consciously choose alternative actions that align with your goals. This technique will be crucial in breaking free from old patterns and forging new, healthier habits.

So, as we go further into these powerful concepts in our journaling, remember that they're here to support your journey to change.

MET Prioritization

Start by listing your top priorities in your life, such as family, career, self-development, health, and spirituality. Reflect on why these aspects are important and how your alcohol consumption may have affected them. Writing about these priorities will deepen your understanding of their significance and reinforce your motivation for a healthier life.

Once you've established your priorities, consider the actions you can take to achieve your goals in each area. These actions might include spending more quality time with family, pursuing professional development opportunities, or committing to a healthier lifestyle. By identifying and documenting the necessary steps, you'll create a sense of accountability and direction, empowering you to make meaningful progress in all aspects of your life.

CBT and Triggers

Do you have the urge to drink? If this is the case, a simple reflection in answering with none will add to our cumulative effect that you are strengthening your resolve to part from alcohol. However, no matter who you are and how strong your resolve is, instances are bound to arise that may test that resolve. Generally, my urges are at zero on a scale of one to 10. Sometimes they are at two to three. In those instances, I must take note of two things: what caused my urge and when these occurred. Usually, these will arise for two reasons.

The first is a trigger, an external stimulus often coming out of nowhere. For example, you pass by your favorite liquor store on the way home, which causes you to reminisce about your favorite bottle of wine or cocktail. Or you could be sitting on your couch, having a great day, and having plans for the following morning. For some reason, you start thinking it might be nice to have a drink. Triggers and urges overlap in their roots, but I like to break them apart for my purposes here.

If you find yourself regularly triggered by an external factor, it's important to note what that is. You must identify the trigger, write about how it made you feel, and problem-solve. For example, maybe you find an alternate route home. We typically wouldn't want the inconvenience. But if we take time to see it as a trigger or obstacle, we can also see it as an opportunity. The extra 10 minutes to reroute could give you time to digest a new audiobook without the trigger as a mental distraction. It may initially seem inconvenient, but remember the analogy of death by a thousand paper cuts. The more we can avoid, the stronger we become. Remember as well this isn't about avoidance forever. We are problem-solving to set us up for where we want to go.

Over time, the exact trigger will eventually give way to our internal resolve, and those triggers will disappear. When it comes to urges, it's equally important that we recognize them when they arise and work through them by journaling. Maybe for no reason at all, you'll find yourself having urges. Take time in your journal to address when those urges occurred. Are there any patterns that you can recognize? If it was a great day, maybe celebrating around a bottle is your old default. Perhaps it was a difficult day. This is your old coping default. You will move forward as you are more aware of the when and why of the urge. With that self-awareness, you are prepared to deal with the cravings in the future, especially on a tough day.

HRT and Triggers
Begin by taking note of the situations, people, or emotions that typically lead you to drink. Write these down in your journal and reflect on them. This increased awareness of your triggers will help you better prepare for and handle them without abusing alcohol.

Explore alternative habits you can engage in when facing these triggers. Record these alternatives in your journal, and consider how they might fit into your life. Think about activities, hobbies, or coping strategies to help you manage stress or overcome cravings.

Let's stay with my example of an urge after returning from work and relaxing on the couch. Take time in your journal to observe how you can prevent those urges. Instead of resting on the sofa, you could find activities that fill the void – enjoying a family game night, going for ice cream with the kids, driving to the gym for a sauna, or taking a hot bath. These are only examples. Find ways to change your scenario. Success happens more often when we have a plan. And journaling is the tool to create this success.

This example of a journal entry is a very simple one. Think about your day and find at least one improvement by no longer drinking. Some examples could be waking up an hour earlier, running faster and further on your job, sticking to your diet, and spending time with your family. There's no limit to what we can do with this thing called journaling. It can be one thing or ten or more. We are connecting the idea that being alcohol-free equals joy and growth. You'll find this the reality when you review your day and see all the wonderful improvements you are making in all areas with your newfound commitment.

You take the time daily to insert a to-do or reaffirm your work in each area of your life. Again, these guidelines are for your journal. There is no set format, but what gets measured gets done. Some of these may be daily tasks, others long-term goals. As you work on this section, attend to your progress. Are you moving forward, or are you going through the motions of putting items on the list? If you find one of your priorities is not progressing, then why? When this happens, ask yourself what keeps you from achieving this goal or to-do. Does it belong? It's possible the goal is not a priority. If that's the case, refresh your top-level objectives and grab a new ball to run with. It's okay, as long as procrastination is not the reason. We tend to give importance to career or work, but if you do not attend to other areas of your life, I can promise they will all suffer, including the areas that get the most focus. Wholeness is the key to growth.

Overview:

- Journal Framework: journal for personal growth and self-reflection, no formal rules
- Gratitude: start with gratitude to improve positivity, happiness, and self-esteem
- Recent Wins: acknowledge small accomplishments to boost confidence and motivation
- Triggers and Urges: identify and address external triggers and internal urges related to alcohol
- Daily Improvements: connect alcohol-free living with positive changes in life
- Prioritization: focus on top priorities in different areas of life (family, career, self-development, health, spiritual)
- Progress Evaluation: assess progress in each priority area and make adjustments if needed

SCRUM Method

"Success is the sum of small efforts, repeated day in and day out."

- ROBERT COLLIER.

One Day at a Time

At first, refraining from alcohol may seem insurmountable. Let's say you are on day two. Thinking of abstaining for 64 more days will feel like a big task. If we look at it just for today, then it feels manageable. There is neurological science that backs up the principle. A study published in the *American Journal of Psychology* reported findings from brain imaging one day to two weeks after the initial abstinence from alcohol. The study looked at the level of disruption between the ventral medial prefrontal cortex and striatum, the network linked to decision-making. They concluded that the more recent the last drink, the greater the likelihood that an individual would resume drinking. They also concluded that the severity of the disruptions between these two brain regions diminished with increased abstinence.

The science behind the principle of one day at a time is meaningful. On a difficult day, we win if we know we can make it to the next. Scientific research tells us the next day will be easier than today. What I haven't mentioned is how much more effortless your abstinence becomes. The data is compelling. During the first 14 days, researchers found disruptions were at their highest. However, with each additional day of abstinence during that period, the upsets, on average, decreased by 14%. That's incredible. Think about the compounding effect of your daily improvement. Embracing that day-by-day abstinence gets more manageable, we can build that momentum to add more than one day into real change. (Source)

The most improvement occurs in the first week and continues to diminish over two weeks. In addition to pushing forward daily, we will include a week-by-week strategy. Aside from making a perceivable new section, the scrum framework in rugby, the team comes together in what they call a scrum to work together to move the ball forward.

I work in software where the term Scrum has been borrowed from rugby used to describe the formation of players. Scrum (Systematic Customer Resolution Unraveling Meeting (scrum.org) is a methodology term in data analysis. Scrum breaks down large projects in sprints of manageable time increments, generally in one to two weeks. The framework helps guide and manage work through values, principles, and practices, like a rugby team training for the big game. Scrum encourages us to learn through experiences of self-organization while continuing to work on a problem and reflecting on the wins and losses to improve. The same principle is applied when taking on a big task by chunking it into smaller increments. We can apply Scrum to modify our habits around alcohol. Instead of looking at 66 days as a whole, one day at a time in between, we will use a framework instead. The framework will be broken down by daily progress, accountability, weekly sprints, and monthly reviews. Aside from making a project smaller, we can make micro-adjustments along the way for our unforeseen goal obstacles. This will allow us to use daily and weekly reviews of what we worked on, what went well, and what didn't. We can review and adjust the course in small increments, making it much less likely to get off course.

The Scrum framework provides a flexible developmental process. I adapted the framework to suit our goals with habit formation. I break down the three pillars of how we will look at the timeline framework and statement of purpose. Explorers have always used the North Star as their guide. These explorers were unaware of the challenges they would encounter on their way to their destination. They had to put one foot in front of the other on the journey and deal with the obstacles as they occurred. But one thing is certain: they focused on their destination. So too, we focus on our destination --our statement of purpose to achieve alcohol abstinence in 66 days.

The Weekly Sprint Plan
Sprint planning allows you to observe the next seven days. We will break it down further into our daily standup, the planning day. This enables you to monitor how your week went and what lies ahead. Let's say you have a

heavier workload this week. How do you plan to handle the end of those days so you don't end them with a drink? Maybe you have a work event or family party that week. The easiest way to break a habit is to replace it with a new one. For me, it was fitness, rising early to mountain bike. During your planning period, take the time to map out your week. It doesn't have to be an extensive checklist and agenda. The goal here is forethought.

- Vision: Write down your vision and what you intend to achieve through this work. This is an overall affirmation, not just for the week.
- Challenges: Write down the challenges for the week, either external or internal.
- Estimate the workload: Some weeks will be easy; you may sense that from the beginning. Some weeks may be busy and a little chaotic. Be mindful of the causes and record what you anticipate.
- Commit: Reaffirm your commitment. Verbalizing our commitment empowers our minds and actions. This is your time to say, let's do it!

The Daily Standup
The daily standup is an example. We use Scrum for planning and execution on a daily time block. Our daily standup will be our journaling. This is your time to review and reflect on the previous day, how you plan the current day, and what obstacles you may see ahead. It also could be a time to reach out to your accountability partner, especially when you see barriers. This forethought allows us to review and plan daily and explains why journaling is a core foundation for achieving our goals. Use the journal framework as your daily standup.

Weekly Review
Congrats, you've made it. The weekly review is the time to observe how the week went. Your daily thoughts and challenges can be lost even briefly. Luckily, you have your journal with daily standup notes. I invite you to take more time on this day for review and reflection. Look back through your journal entries. Read through where you might recognize both the

winning points and the challenges. Was it easy to get through the week? If not, why was it challenging? What specifically was difficult? I've had weeks that were a breeze, and seemingly out of nowhere, I had a week of challenges and temptations. How difficult those temptations are is usually related to how aware I am. If I've fallen back into old habits, it usually is because I haven't taken the time to review and plan for them. Even if everything seems easy, you need to be aware. If things are challenging, you will be up for the challenge if you review and plan for the next step.

After the weekly review, I want you to set up a reward for yourself that motivates you. In my case, I calculated what I would spend on alcohol in a typical week ($80 to $100) and then decided how to reward myself with the money saved. Sometimes I would use the savings to buy clothing I usually would not buy as I'm notoriously frugal in this area. Sometimes it would be mountain bike gear or taking the kids for a night out of fun. You may want to save up for a bigger reward. In that event, I suggest a money jar so that you can see something tangible. I will go into more in detail about this later in the book. Placing the cash in a jar and seeing it accrue has the same reward effect. This is because its free, money regained, and yours to enjoy as a reward for a better lifestyle.

Weekly Retrospective
The weekly and retro reviews go hand in hand. With your review, you will re-observe all that has happened over the week. The retro is where we dive deeper. We uncover what worked and what didn't. It is the time to problem-solve and improve for the upcoming week.

We can solve the problems by drawing on the strengths you have identified through your review. For example, where did you feel the strongest this week and why? What challenges did you face? Why did those occur? What instances this week could you have handled better? Why do you think you could have done better?

Now it is time to brainstorm solutions. This is a free-form session to look at the questions you have asked yourself. You may have identified a challenging situation. You have analyzed why it was tough. Now is the time to brainstorm ways that you can address the problem should it arise again. Maybe you remove yourself from future situations, such as a social function with alcohol. Perhaps it is reducing your workload stress. As you explore, write your solutions to these challenges. As a reminder, writing your observations of your struggles is a powerful tool to move beyond your ordinary day-to-day life. In committing your resolve to paper, you position yourself for growth and success.

Section	General Idea	Action Points
The Weekly Sprint Planning	Plan your week to be more mindful of your habits and goals.	1. Write down your vision. 2. List challenges. 3. Estimate workload. 4. Commit to your plan.
The Daily Standup	Reflect on your progress and obstacles every day through journaling.	Use the Journal framework for daily reflection and planning.
Weekly Review	Analyze your week's progress and challenges by reviewing your journal entries.	1. Reflect on your week. 2. Identify successes and challenges. 3. Plan rewards for achievements.
Weekly Retrospective	Dive deeper into the week's experiences to identify areas for improvement and strategize for the upcoming week.	1. Analyze your strengths and weaknesses. 2. Identify challenges and their causes. 3. Brainstorm solutions.

Overview:

- Adapt Scrum framework for habit formation and alcohol abstinence
- Three pillars: timeline framework, statement of purpose, and 66-day goal
- Weekly Sprint Plan: Observe the upcoming week, plan for challenges, and reaffirm commitment
- Daily Standup: Use journaling for daily reflection and planning
- Weekly Review: Analyze the week's successes and challenges; plan for the next step
- Weekly Reward: Treat yourself with money saved from not drinking alcohol
- Weekly Retrospective: Dive deeper into what worked and what didn't; brainstorm solutions for improvement

R.E.S.E.T. Guidebook

To enhance your journey, I've created a comprehensive guidebook. It serves as a practical companion to the book, making it easier for you to put the concepts into action. Get your copy at hardenbrook.com/nwr or scan the QR code.

Habit Swapping

"The best way to break a bad habit is to replace it with a good one."

- JACK DIXON.

In an earlier chapter, we discussed the habit loop, which consists of cues, routines, and rewards. To briefly remind you about the habit loop, it involves:

Cue: The trigger that tells your brain to go into automatic mode and perform the behavior.
Routine. The behavior itself.
Reward: The satisfaction or pleasure that you get from completing the behavior.

The habit loop is a powerful tool to create or break habits. Now, let's apply this knowledge to the concept of habit swapping. Habit swapping is about replacing an existing routine with a new, healthier one while keeping the same cue and reward. A study by Wood and Neal (2007) found that people who used habit-replacement strategies experienced greater success in changing their habits than those who didn't.

Every choice we make, conscious or not, lays down a neural pathway. The more we tread on this pathway, the stronger and more automatic it becomes. But the beauty of our brain's architecture is its flexibility. We can pave new paths with commitment and consistency, ensuring our habits align with our goals.

Action Steps:

Identify Existing Habits: Recognize the routines you engage in daily. Which ones serve you, and which ones impede your progress? Let's focus on the latter.

Pinpoint the Cue and Reward: For each habit you wish to change, clearly define its cue and reward. This clarity lays the foundation for successful habit swapping.

Brainstorm New Routines: Think about routines that can provide the same reward but are healthier or more aligned with your goals.

Commit and Practice: Replace the old routine with the new one consistently. It might require conscious effort early on, but the new routine will change your habits with time.

Reflect and Adjust: Regularly check in with yourself. How is the new routine serving you? If something isn't working, tweak it. Remember, this is a journey, not a destination. Flexibility is key.

Now, let's explore how we can apply this knowledge to help us swap out our routines around drinking.

Example 1: Swap Fitness

Imagine that you usually have a drink to de-stress after a particularly tough day at work. The cue is stress, the routine is drinking, and the reward is relaxation. You could use a yoga session instead of reaching for that drink to swap this habit. Yoga is known for its stress-relieving benefits, and it can help you feel calmer and more centered. So, in this case, the cue remains the same – stress from work – and the reward is still relaxation. Still, you've swapped the routine to practicing yoga, a healthier alternative. Over time, your brain will form a connection between the new routine and the same reward, making it easier to maintain this habit.

Example 2: Swap Family Time

Let's say you're in the habit of having a drink while watching TV with your family in the evening. The cue is the evening family time, the routine is drinking, and the reward is bonding with your loved ones. You could initiate a family game night instead to swap this habit. Choose a board, card, or video game everyone can enjoy together. This way, the cue remains the same – evening family time – and the reward is still bonding with your family. Still, you've swapped the routine to playing games

NO WILLPOWER REQUIRED | 115

together, a more engaging and wholesome activity. As you continue this new routine, your brain will start associating family time with the fun and connection of game night rather than drinking, reinforcing the new habit.

Example 3: Swap Beverage Alternative

Suppose you have a nightly routine of unwinding with a glass of wine before bed. The cue is the desire to relax at the end of the day; the routine is drinking wine, and the reward is the feeling of relaxation. To swap this habit, try kava instead of wine. Kava, a beverage made from kava plant roots, is known for its calming and relaxing effects without causing intoxication.

In this habit swap, the cue remains the same – the desire to relax at the end of the day – and the reward is still relaxation. You've swapped the routine to drinking kava, which offers a similar calming effect without the downsides of alcohol. As you consistently replace your nightly glass of wine with kava, your brain will associate the new routine with the same reward of relaxation, helping you establish and maintain this healthier habit.

The key to success with habit swapping is consistency and persistence. Keep practicing the new routine in response to the same cue, and over time, your brain will strengthen the neural connections associated with the new habit. Remember, we're all in this together, and I'm here to support you.

Overview:

- Habit loop: consists of cue, routine, and reward.
- Habit-swapping: replacing existing routine with a healthier one while keeping cue and reward
- Neuroscience: understanding it improves habit-swapping success
- Example 1: Swap Fitness - replace drinking with yoga for stress relief.
- Example 2: Swap Family Time - replace drinking with family game night for bonding.
- Example 3: Swap Beverage Alternative - replace wine with kava for relaxation.
- Key to success: consistency and persistence in practicing a new routine.

Urge Surfing

"You can't stop the waves, but you can learn to surf."

\- JON KABAT-ZINN.

Urge surfing is a mindfulness-based technique that helps cope with cravings and urges by accepting and observing them rather than trying to suppress or ignore them. It involves focusing on the sensations and emotions associated with a craving, allowing them to be fully experienced without resistance. Instead of fighting or avoiding the urge, you learn to "ride the wave" by observing and accepting the craving as a temporary, fluctuating experience.

The late Dr. Alan Marlatt, a renowned psychologist and addictions researcher, focused on developing "urge surfing," i.e., harm reduction and relapse prevention strategies for individuals struggling with addictive behaviors. He recognized that suppressing cravings could often backfire, leading to increased urges.

When practicing urge surfing, you accept cravings as a normal and natural part of recovery. By acknowledging these urges without judgment, you can break the cycle of guilt and shame that often perpetuates addictive behaviors.

Here's a hypothetical situation of how you can put to practice in situations where you may find yourself tempted and how to counter those urges. It had been years since Tom had seen his college friends, and now they were gathering for a long-overdue reunion weekend at a cozy cabin in the mountains. Tom has come a long way since those wild college days. Over the past month, he had made significant progress in his commitment to take a break from alcohol. He was determined to maintain his newfound balance during the reunion.

As his friends reminisced and laughter filled the cabin, someone opened a bottle of Tom's favorite whiskey. The familiar scent filled the air, and Tom could feel the temptation to join in growing stronger.

Tom knew he had to act fast to keep his cravings in check. He acknowledged his craving for alcohol without judgment or shame, facing it head-on by practicing urge surfing. He excused himself from the group, found a quiet corner, and took a deep breath to center himself.

As Tom focused on his breath, he began to visualize his craving as a powerful wave. He could see the wave growing, reaching its peak, and eventually subsiding, just as urges do. He reminded himself that, like waves, cravings are temporary, and he had the power to ride them out without being swept away.

Tom continued to breathe deeply, concentrating on the physical sensations in his body. He noticed the tightness in his chest and the warmth in his face as the urge intensified. With each breath, he acknowledged these sensations, allowing them to be present without trying to fight or suppress them. Gradually, Tom could feel the intensity of his craving begins to diminish. He rode the wave as it subsided, and he felt a renewed sense of control and determination.

Having successfully navigated the storm of temptation, Tom rejoined the group, confident in his ability to enjoy the evening without alcohol. He poured himself a glass of sparkling water and toasted with his friends, feeling proud of his accomplishment.

Throughout the weekend, Tom continued to use urge surfing whenever he felt tempted to drink. By facing his cravings head-on and riding the waves, he maintained his commitment to sobriety and enjoyed the reunion without compromising his progress.

Tom's fictional journey illustrates the power of urge surfing in managing cravings and staying true to one's goals. By acknowledging and observing urges without judgment, individuals can learn to ride the waves of temptation and maintain control over their choices. Here's a step-by-step guide on how to practice urge surfing:

Acknowledge the Urge: When you notice a craving or an urge, acknowledge its presence without judgment. Recognize that the urge is a natural part of your experience, and try not to label it as good or bad.

Find a Comfortable Position: Choose a comfortable seated or lying position, ideally in a quiet space. Close your eyes or maintain a soft gaze to minimize distractions.

Focus on Your Breath: Bring your attention to your breath, observing its natural rhythm without trying to change it. Notice the sensation of air flowing in and out of your nostrils, the rise and fall of your chest and abdomen, and any other sensations associated with breathing.

Observe the Urge: Shift your attention to the craving or urge itself. Observe its intensity, quality, and location in your body. Are there any physical sensations associated with the urge, such as tightness, heat, or discomfort? Be curious about these sensations without trying to change or resist them.

Surf the Urge: As you continue to observe the urge, imagine it as a wave in the ocean. Visualize yourself surfing on top of the wave, riding its peaks and troughs without being consumed by it. Remember that, like waves, urges rise and fall, eventually dissipating.

Practice Acceptance: As you surf the urge, practice acceptance and non-judgment. Recognize that it's normal to have urges and that resisting or fighting them often makes them stronger. By accepting the urge and allowing it to pass, you can reduce its power over you.

Refocus on Your Breath: When the urge has subsided, or you feel ready to move on, gently shift your focus back to your breath. Take a few deep, slow breaths to ground yourself in the present moment.

Reflect and learn: Once the exercise is over, take some time to reflect on your experience. What did you learn about your urge, and how did it change over time? Were there any insights or realizations that emerged during your practice?

Practice regularly: Urge surfing is a skill that improves with practice. Incorporate it into your daily routine or use it whenever you experience a craving or strong urge. Over time, you may find that your ability to manage urges improves, leading to greater self-control and resilience.

Remember, being patient with yourself is essential as you learn and practice urge surfing. It may take time to become comfortable with this technique, but it can become an effective tool for managing cravings and urges with consistent practice.

Overview:

- Urge surfing: a mindfulness-based technique for coping with cravings and urges.
- Accept and observe: experience sensations and emotions without resistance.
- Acknowledging urges without judgment breaks the cycle of guilt.
- Step-by-step guide: acknowledge the urge, find a comfortable position, focus on your breath, observe the urge, surf the urge, practice acceptance, refocus on your breath, reflect, and learn.
- Practice regularly: consistent practice leads to greater self-control and resilience.
- Patience: allow time for you to become comfortable with the technique.

Drinking Ritual

"Rituals are the formulas by which harmony is restored."

- TERRY TEMPEST WILLIAMS.

For many people, a drink after work or while relaxing on the beach has become synonymous with relaxation and enjoyment. However, when trying to control or quit alcohol consumption, it's important to replace that alcoholic drink with a NA alternative. We'll explore why attaching enjoyment to NA drinks is essential in successfully replacing old habits and how visualization techniques can help reinforce this new sense of attachment.

Replacing the old habit with a new, healthier one is crucial. Doing so makes you more likely to stick to your new routine, as it will satisfy the exact emotional and psychological needs that the previous habit fulfilled. By attaching enjoyment to a NA drink, you can still experience pleasure and relaxation without the negative consequences of alcohol consumption. This process creates new neural pathways in the brain, helping to overwrite the old connections between alcohol and enjoyment.

Visualization is a powerful tool that can help reinforce the new association between NA drinks and enjoyment. By vividly imagining the pleasure of sipping a refreshing beverage on the beach or after a long day at work, you strengthen the emotional connection to the new habit. For me, it's sparkling water –specifically, an ice-cold Topo Chico with a lime. I love the bottle's look, with the condensation running down on the outside and watching the carbonation bubble up to the lime floating in the bottle. To me, this becomes the trigger of relaxation and enjoyment. I begin to crave it. The best part is it's healthy! On a hot day, there's nothing more refreshing.

Choose a NA drink that you find appealing and refreshing –perhaps a mocktail, sparkling water, or any other beverage you enjoy. Identify the occasions when you would typically consume an alcoholic drink. Visualize yourself in these situations, enjoying the NA drink. Imagine the taste, the sensation of the cold glass in your hand, and the feeling of refreshment as you take a sip.

As you envision this scenario, focus on the positive emotions and sensations that the NA drink evokes. This could include feelings of relaxation, satisfaction, and even pride in your healthier choice. By consistently practicing this visualization technique, you'll create a strong mental association between NA drinks and enjoyment, making it easier to embrace this new habit.

Sparkling Water: Sparkling water is a timeless NA alternative that offers a refreshing and hydrating option. You can enjoy it plain or add a splash of natural flavor with a slice of lemon, lime, or cucumber. Add a few drops of bitters or a splash of flavored syrup for a more sophisticated touch.

Mocktails: Mocktails are NA versions of popular cocktails, allowing you to indulge in the taste and presentation of your favorite drinks without the alcohol.

Kava: Kava is a traditional drink from the South Pacific made from the kava plant's roots. It is known for its calming and relaxing effects, making it a popular choice for those seeking a NA drink with a bit of a kick. Kava bars are becoming more widespread, offering a unique and social atmosphere for people to enjoy this earthy, ceremonial beverage.

NA Beer and Wine: Familiar Favorites: The NA beer and wine market has exploded in recent years, with more brands and options available. These beverages undergo a process that removes the alcohol while maintaining the flavor and body of their alcoholic counterparts. You can enjoy the taste of your favorite beer or wine without the side effects of alcohol.

Kombucha: Kombucha is a fermented tea drink with a tangy, slightly sweet flavor and a gentle fizz. Rich in probiotics, it's a healthy alternative to alcohol that can aid digestion and boost gut health. Kombucha comes in various flavors, from fruity to herbal, and is on tap at some bars and restaurants.

Craft Sodas: Craft sodas are artisanal, small-batch beverages with high-quality ingredients and unique flavor combinations. With a focus on natural flavors and less sugar than traditional sodas, they offer a more sophisticated and healthier alternative to alcohol. Some popular craft soda flavors include lavender lemonade, hibiscus ginger, and elderflower.

By attaching enjoyment to NA drinks and using visualization techniques, you can rewire your brain to associate pleasure and relaxation with healthier choices. Over time, this new habit will become second nature, allowing you to enjoy life's special moments without alcohol.

Overview:

- Attaching enjoyment to NA drinks is essential to successfully replacing a habit.
- Replacing old habits with healthier ones fulfills emotional and psychological needs.
- Visualization strengthens the emotional connection to the new habit.
- Choose sparkling water, mocktails, kava, NA beer and wine, kombucha, and craft sodas as NA alternatives.
- Visualize enjoying a NA drink in situations where you'd typically consume alcohol.
- Focus on positive emotions and sensations during visualization.
- Rewiring the brain associates pleasure and relaxation with healthier choices.
- The new habit becomes second nature over time, allowing enjoyment without alcohol.

Reward Visualization

"Visualization is daydreaming with a purpose."

- BO BENNETT.

In a previous chapter, we discussed the power of using a reward system to reinforce your decision to take a break from alcohol. Now, we will kick things up a notch and make those rewards tangible so you can see and touch the fruits of your determination. This chapter is about creating a visual money jar to help reset your habits and spark creative motivation during your 66-day alcohol-free journey.

The Power of Visualization

There's something special about the difference between mentally calculating how much money you save by not drinking and physically seeing that amount accumulate in front of your eyes. Visualization is a powerful tool for manifesting your goals, and by creating a visual money jar, you're strengthening your commitment to your alcohol-free journey. In fact, research has shown that visualization can activate the same neural networks as actually performing an action, which can lead to better performance and outcomes (Guillot & Collet, 2008).

Creating Your Visual Money Jar

Here's what I want you to do: head over to your bank and withdraw the amount of money you would've spent on alcohol for the week. Hold it in your hands and feel the weight of your accomplishment. Next, find a transparent container—a jar, a vase, or any other creative receptacle—where you can stash your money. Feel free to personalize your money jar with labels like "Fun Money" or "My Reward" to crank up the excitement.

Every day, take out the amount you would've spent on alcohol and consciously place it in your money jar. Put the container in a prominent spot where you can see it throughout the day. As the money piles up over the week, you'll see the rewards and benefits waiting for you.

Celebrate Your Success

How you choose to celebrate your success is entirely up to you. You can treat yourself to something special each week or even give a gift to someone else if that brings you more joy. Alternatively, you can let your money jar grow for the entire 66 days, allowing the anticipation and satisfaction of watching your savings increase to fuel your motivation. The choice is yours, and there's no right or wrong way to reward yourself.

Visualization is a powerful tool for manifesting goals:

The main goal of this exercise is to create a physical action and reminder that reinforces your new, positive habits. By actively participating in the growth of your money jar, you'll be encouraged to stay the course during your 66-day break from alcohol. This visual representation of your progress will constantly remind you of your transformation and the rewards that come with it.

Overview:

- Create a visual money jar by putting the money saved from not drinking in a transparent container.
- Personalize your money jar to increase excitement and motivation.
- Place the container in a prominent spot as a daily reminder of your progress.
- Celebrate your success by treating yourself or others with your saved money.
- The purpose of the visual money jar is to reinforce new, positive habits and motivate you during your 66-day alcohol-free journey.
- This physical reminder encourages you to stay committed and reminds you of the rewards of your transformation.

EFT Tapping

"EFT is a simple yet powerful tool for transforming emotional pain into peace."

- DEEPAK CHOPRA.

Emotional Freedom Technique (EFT) tapping is an effective self-help method that combines aspects of acupressure and psychology to address emotional and physical concerns. In recent years, it has emerged as an effective way to manage stress, anxiety, and cravings, including those associated with the desire for alcohol. This chapter outlines best practices for using EFT tapping to manage cravings and support healthier habits successfully.

Identify the Craving or Trigger: Before starting an EFT tapping session, take a moment to pinpoint the specific craving or trigger you want to tackle. This may involve recognizing the emotions, thoughts, or physical sensations related to the craving. A clear understanding of the issue will help you address it more effectively during tapping.

Develop a Setup Statement: A setup statement is a verbal affirmation acknowledging the issue you are addressing while expressing self-acceptance. For example, "Even though I have this strong craving for alcohol, I deeply and completely accept myself." Repeat this statement three times while tapping on the side of your hand, also known as the karate chop point.

Create Reminder Phrases: Reminder phrases are concise descriptions of the issue that help you stay focused while tapping on each acupressure point. For example, "this alcohol craving" or "this urge to drink." Repeat these phrases as you tap on each point.

Follow the Tapping Sequence: There is a specific sequence of acupressure points to tap on during EFT. These points include:

1. The eyebrow (inner edge)
2. Side of the eye
3. Under the eye
4. Under the nose
5. Chin (between the lower lip and chin)
6. Collarbone
7. Under the arm (about 4 inches below the armpit)
8. Top of the head

Use two or three fingers to tap each point gently but firmly about 5-7 times while repeating the reminder phrases.

Evaluate Your Progress: After completing one round of tapping, assess your craving or emotional intensity on a scale of 1-10. If your intensity has decreased but has not disappeared, continue tapping for additional rounds, adjusting the setup statement and reminder phrases to reflect your progress.

Practice Regularly: Consistent practice is essential for maximizing the benefits of EFT tapping. Establish a routine and allocate time for daily or weekly tapping sessions to build and maintain momentum in managing cravings.

Overview:

- EFT tapping is a self-help method that addresses emotional and physical concerns.
- Pinpointing the specific craving or trigger you want to address.
- Develop a setup statement that acknowledges the issue and self-acceptance.
- Create concise reminder phrases to stay focused on.
- Follow a specific sequence of acupressure points while tapping and repeating reminder phrases.
- After one round of tapping, evaluate your craving or emotional intensity and adjust as needed.
- Practice EFT tapping consistently to maximize benefits and manage cravings.

PART
05

Mind & Body Support

| Personalized Pathways

Throughout this book, we've established the foundation for habit change with alcohol, focusing on essential techniques and strategies crucial for creating lasting transformation. As we move into section five and six of the book, I want to emphasize that altering your habits with alcohol is an incredibly personal journey. Each person's relationship with alcohol is unique, influenced by individual stages in life, personality traits, personal histories, and connections. As a result, there is no one-size-fits-all approach to addressing our habits with alcohol.

The additional techniques and tools presented in this book aim to support and strengthen the changes you've made so far. However, not all of these supplemental strategies will be necessary for everyone. It's not my intention for you to adopt all of these techniques; instead, I encourage you to choose one or two that resonate with you and seem appealing. For example, while I struggle with traditional meditation, I find breathwork beneficial, as it allows me to achieve the mindfulness that meditation can provide.

With a shift in mindset around why you drink, the practice of journaling, and enlisting someone for accountability, you should be able to achieve your goals within 66 days. However, if you desire more support or need additional assistance with mindfulness and caring for your body, I've included these tools—most of which I use regularly—to help reinforce your new commitment.

As you reflect on the techniques and concepts presented throughout this book, I encourage you to take a personalized approach to your journey. Choose the strategies that resonate with you and feel most compatible with your unique situation. Remember that it's entirely up to you to shape your path, and it's important to make choices that align with your individual circumstances and goals. By tailoring your approach to habit change, you can increase your chances of success and build a healthier, more fulfilling relationship with alcohol.

The Supplement Guide

"Take care of your body. It's the only place you have to live."

- JIM ROHN.

The Doctor

In the upcoming chapter and supplement guide, we have the privilege of featuring the expert advice of Dr. Robin Terranella, a highly respected naturopathic doctor. Dr. Terranella received his medical training at the esteemed Bastyr University of Naturopathic Medicine, which is renowned for its rigorous curriculum and emphasis on holistic healing. With a wealth of experience and knowledge, Dr. Terranella skillfully combines Eastern and Western medicine, offering his patients a comprehensive range of both alternative and conventional treatment options. As an authority in the field, Dr. Terranella is uniquely equipped to guide us through the process, providing invaluable physical and mental support during this critical period.

The Guide

Our body is a complex system of competing signals from tissues and organ systems. These signals come from the food we eat, the air we breathe, our thought patterns, the things we drink, and the things generated internally from our bodies. Some signals are very static, while others change from day to day. We can think of the ebbs and flows of these various signals as our homeostatic set point. Our bodies are always trying to keep things in homeostasis. However, homeostasis is not static either; it is a range. So, you might have a homeostatic set point for your testosterone of 700 ng/dl output on any given day. One day it may be 775, and another day might be 650. Your body is trying to keep it at 700, sometimes more or less.

This type of thing happens with all the molecules in our bodies every second of every day. Your body is trying to maintain this balance. Some of these biochemicals are kept in a tighter range than others, but the principle of homeostasis regulates all. We can think of this as a steady state. Anything outside of the normal will alter the homeostasis of your body. As a result, your body will try to re-establish its steady state using its internal regulatory systems.

When you drink alcohol, even a little, you disrupt the body's homeostasis. The more you drink, the more consistently these regulatory systems kick in. Symptoms and cravings come from these regulatory systems, at least in the acute stage. When you stop drinking, even if it was just a one-night thing, your body tries to counteract the sedative effects of alcohol by stimulating you. This counteraction is why people feel anxious the next day and often wake up early, shaky and sweaty. The sedation side of our nervous system gets pushed way too far out from its set point with alcohol. The body counteracts this by producing stimulating neurotransmitters and chemicals. Now, this counteracting effect has consequences too. It uses up resources and generally taxes the body. The more you tax the body, the longer it will take for the body to recover. There are specific principles and approaches one can take to help the body heal and re-establish balance, which we will discuss below.

Equally important is the effect of alcohol on the absorption and utilization of certain key vitamins and nutrients. Alcohol causes the depletion of vitamin B1, also known as thiamine. The long-term regular use of alcohol can lead to something known as Wernicke-Korsakoff encephalitis, a form of dementia that happens because the body cannot get enough vitamin B1 due to the consumption of alcohol. Now, you don't need to be an alcoholic to become thiamine deficient. There are dietary choices that lead to thiamine deficiency independent of alcohol consumption. Some people have genetic alterations that cause their bodies to need more thiamine. In a susceptible individual, this becomes even more important.

Other essential nutrients that can be affected by alcohol consumption include vitamin B12 and magnesium. Consider incorporating higher protein in your diet to support your body's general health, neurotransmitters, and mood –0.5 grams per pound of body weight is recommended. This supplementation will give your body amino acids to make neurotransmitters (see tyrosine and tryptophan). Also, consider incorporating omega-3s and the herb mucuna into your supplement regimen.

The Essentials

Our curated supplement stack is designed to support your body's return to its natural state of balance and equilibrium, known as homeostasis. Start with the essentials list—it's your starting point. If you find the need for extra support, explore the labeled sections that align with your specific symptoms.

Thiamine (Allithiamine) is crucial for proper brain function and energy metabolism. Alcohol consumption can lead to thiamine deficiency, which can cause neurological problems and cognitive impairment. Allithiamine, a highly bioavailable form of thiamine, helps replenish depleted stores, supports brain function, and reduces the risk of alcohol-related cognitive issues.

B-complex - B vitamins are vital in energy production, neurotransmitter synthesis, and maintaining a healthy nervous system. Alcohol consumption can interfere with the absorption and utilization of B vitamins, leading to deficiencies. Supplementing with a B-complex can help restore normal levels and support overall nervous system health during withdrawal.

Magnesium is an essential mineral involved in over 300 biochemical reactions in the body, including muscle and nerve function, energy production, and stress management. Alcohol can deplete magnesium levels, exacerbating withdrawal symptoms like anxiety, muscle cramps, and irritability. Supplementing with magnesium glycinate or threonate can help restore normal levels and support a smoother withdrawal process.

L-tyrosine is an amino acid that serves as a precursor to several important neurotransmitters, including dopamine, norepinephrine, and epinephrine. These neurotransmitters are often depleted in individuals with a history of alcohol abuse. Supplementing with L-tyrosine can help support the production of these neurotransmitters, improving mood, focus, and overall cognitive function during withdrawal. Start with small doses.

5-HTP is a precursor to serotonin, an essential neurotransmitter in mood regulation, appetite, and sleep. Alcohol abuse can disrupt serotonin levels, leading to withdrawal symptoms like anxiety, depression, and sleep disturbances. Taking 5-HTP during withdrawal can help support healthy serotonin levels and alleviate some symptoms. Start with small doses.

Specifically for Depression Fatigue and Social Anxiety
If you have a predisposition to depression or anxiety, or if you start to notice symptoms of these conditions, consider incorporating the following recommendations.

Mucuna contains L-DOPA, a precursor to dopamine. Supplementing with mucuna can help boost dopamine levels, improving mood and reducing withdrawal-related depression and anxiety. However, it should be used with caution and under the guidance of a healthcare professional, as excessive dopamine can have adverse effects.

L-methylfolate is the active form of folate (vitamin B9) that is more readily used by the body. Folate is crucial in synthesizing serotonin, dopamine, and norepinephrine neurotransmitters. These neurotransmitters are involved in mood regulation and the stress response. By ensuring an adequate supply of L-methylfolate, you support the production of these neurotransmitters, which can help alleviate social anxiety symptoms during alcohol withdrawal. Just be careful not to overdo it. In this case, more is not always better. And too much can lead to more anxiety.

S-adenosylmethionine (SAMe) is a naturally occurring compound in the body involved in various biochemical reactions, including the synthesizing neurotransmitters. Research has shown that SAMe can have antidepressant and anxiolytic (anti-anxiety) effects. By supplementing with SAMe, you can help support the balance of neurotransmitters in your brain, which can help reduce social anxiety symptoms during daytime hours in alcohol withdrawal.

Creatine monohydrate is an amino acid derivative that is primarily known for its role in enhancing physical performance and muscle growth. However, creatine also plays a vital role in brain function by helping regenerate adenosine triphosphate (ATP), the primary energy source for cells. During alcohol withdrawal, the brain may experience increased stress and depleted energy levels. By supplementing with creatine monohydrate, you can support brain energy metabolism and overall cognitive function, which may help alleviate social anxiety symptoms during the daytime.

For Mood Stability, Anxiety and Ruminating Thoughts.
Should you be inclined to experience mood fluctuations, anxiety, or ruminating thoughts, or if you begin to observe signs of these issues, consider incorporating the following recommendations.

Omega-3 fatty acids are essential for brain health and are crucial in reducing inflammation. Alcohol abuse can lead to neuroinflammation and oxidative stress, contributing to withdrawal symptoms and long-term cognitive deficits. Supplementing with omega-3s can help support brain function, reduce inflammation, and promote overall mental well-being during withdrawal.

5-HTP is a precursor to serotonin, an essential neurotransmitter in mood regulation, appetite, and sleep. Alcohol abuse can disrupt serotonin levels, leading to withdrawal symptoms like anxiety, depression, and sleep disturbances. Taking 5-HTP during withdrawal can help support healthy serotonin levels and alleviate some symptoms.

Glycine is an amino acid that acts as a neurotransmitter with inhibitory effects on the central nervous system. It can bind to GABA receptors in the brain which has a calming effect. Glycine has similar but more subtle effects as things like benzodiazepines like valium. This can help promote relaxation, improve sleep quality, and reduce anxiety during alcohol withdrawal. Glycine may also support liver function and detoxification processes, which can be compromised during withdrawal.

For Sleep Issues

If you tend to have sleep disturbances or if you start noticing symptoms of sleep problems, consider incorporating the following recommendations.

L-theanine is an amino acid commonly found in tea leaves. It is known for promoting relaxation without causing drowsiness. L-theanine increases the production of GABA, a neurotransmitter that helps calm the nervous system and reduces feelings of stress and anxiety. It can also help improve sleep quality by promoting relaxation before bedtime.

GABA, short for gamma-aminobutyric acid, is a neurotransmitter that plays a crucial role in reducing excitability in the nervous system. It is a natural calming agent and helps brain cells communicate more effectively. By taking a GABA supplement, you can support your body's natural GABA levels, which can help reduce anxiety and promote relaxation, making it easier to fall asleep and stay asleep.

Valerian is an herb used for centuries to help with sleep and anxiety. It is believed to work by increasing GABA levels in the brain, which calms the nervous system. Valerian can help you relax, fall asleep faster, and improve overall sleep quality. It is a natural alternative to prescription sleep aids.

CBD, or cannabidiol, is a compound in cannabis and hemp plants. It has gained popularity for its potential health benefits, including supporting sleep and anxiety. Unlike THC, the psychoactive compound in marijuana, CBD does not produce a "high." CBD is thought to interact with receptors in the body's endocannabinoid system, which regulates sleep, mood, and stress response. CBD can help promote relaxation, reduce anxiety, and improve sleep quality by influencing the endocannabinoid system.

Cannabinol (CBN) is a mildly psychoactive cannabinoid found in aged cannabis plants due to THC degradation. Although it shares some similarities with CBD, a non-psychoactive compound, CBN has distinct properties and potential health benefits. CBN is more closely associated with aiding sleep and may have more sedative effects.

The Supplementation Schedule

Supplement	Dosage	Frequency	Reason	Additional Instructions
Thiamine	800mg (2-4 weeks), 100mg (2-3 months)	Twice daily	Replenish thiamine levels; support brain function	Adjust duration based on alcohol consumption
B-complex	As directed on the label	As directed on the label	Restore B vitamin levels; support the nervous system	Consult label for specific instructions
Magnesium	300-600mg	Daily	Support muscle & nerve function; stress management	Choose glycinate or threonate chelator
L-tyrosine	500-1000mg	Morning only	Improve mood, focus, and cognitive function	None
Mucuna	500-1000mg	Morning, 2 days off per week	Boost dopamine levels; improve mood	Use with caution; consult a professional
5-HTP	100-200 mg	Evening	Support serotonin levels; alleviate anxiety	None
Glycine	5-10g	Bedtime (during the day as needed)	Promote relaxation; improve sleep quality	None
Omega-3	2g	Daily	Support brain function; reduce inflammation. Mood stabilization	None
L-theanine	200mg	As needed	Promote relaxation; reduce anxiety	None
GABA	1000mg	As needed	Support GABA levels; reduce anxiety	None

Valerian	As directed on the label	Night	Promote relaxation; improve sleep quality	Consult label for specific instructions
CBD	As directed on the label	Night	Reduce anxiety; improve sleep quality	Consult label for specific instructions
L-methylfolate	400mcg-2mg	Daily (AM better)	Support social anxiety relief	None
SAMe	200mg	Daily	Support social anxiety relief	None
Creatine Monohydrate	5 grams	Daily	Support social anxiety relief	Consult label for specific instructions

Streamlining Your Solution:

I've teamed up with Dr. Terranella to offer a more straightforward and cost-effective alternative to buying these supplements individually. For the latest details, visit hardenbrook.com/nwr.

Overview:

- Alcohol disrupts homeostasis: drinking affects the body's balance, causing symptoms and cravings.
- Counteracting sedative effects: the body produces stimulating neurotransmitters and chemicals.
- Alcohol impacts nutrient absorption: depletes essential vitamins and nutrients like vitamin B1 (thiamine).
- Susceptible individuals: Some people are more prone to deficiencies due to genetics or dietary choices.

Sleep Science

"Sleep is the golden chain that ties health and our bodies together."

- THOMAS DEKKER.

It's no secret that alcohol interferes with our sleep quality, preventing us from reaching the deep, restorative stages of sleep that our bodies need to function optimally. By removing alcohol, you'll notice improved sleep quality, duration, and overall well-being.

The Science of Sleep and Alcohol
To understand the positive impact of taking a break from alcohol on your sleep, let's examine the science behind it. Alcohol affects sleep in several ways, primarily by disrupting our sleep-wake cycle and interfering with the production of melatonin, a hormone responsible for regulating sleep (Chan et al., 2013). Additionally, alcohol reduces rapid eye movement (REM) sleep, essential for memory consolidation and emotional processing (Roehrs & Roth, 2001).

The Timeline: When to Expect Improvements
While each person's experience may differ, you can generally expect improvements in your sleep after a few days to a couple of weeks of abstaining from alcohol. A study by Roehrs et al. (1996) found that abstaining from alcohol for just three days improved sleep quality in social drinkers. A more recent study by Colrain et al. (2014) showed significant improvements in sleep quality and brain function after five weeks of abstinence in moderate drinkers.

Navigating the Transition: What to Expect
As you take a break from alcohol, you might experience some sleep disturbances during the initial days or weeks. These disruptions are a natural part of your body's adjustment to the absence of alcohol, and they

should subside as you continue to abstain. Here's a rough timeline of what you can expect:

The first few days: You may experience difficulty falling asleep, staying asleep, or both due to the sudden withdrawal of alcohol's sedative effects on your nervous system. Stay patient and know that this phase is temporary.

One to two weeks: Your sleep should start to stabilize as your body adjusts to the absence of alcohol. You may notice longer and more consistent sleep durations and improved sleep quality.

Three weeks and beyond: By this point, you should be experiencing more restorative sleep, with increased REM and deep sleep stages. You'll feel refreshed and alert during the day as your brain benefits from improved sleep quality.

Overview:

- Alcohol negatively affects sleep quality by disrupting the sleep-wake cycle and interfering with melatonin production.
- Abstaining from alcohol can improve sleep quality, duration, and overall well-being.
- Sleep improvements typically begin after a few days to a couple of weeks of alcohol abstinence.
- Initial sleep disturbances are normal as your body adjusts to the absence of alcohol.
- Sleep improvements continue with time, leading to more restorative sleep and increased alertness.
- Consider supplementation to reduce transition symptoms (details in the book).

NSDR

"Peace comes from within. Do not seek it without."

- GAUTAMA BUDDHA

As in-between drinkers, we sometimes face challenges recovering our body and mind regarding sleep disturbances. One highly effective tool that can help us during this transitional period is Non-Sleep Deep Rest (NSDR) and Yoga Nidra. This powerful practice can help restore the mind and body while they return to a state of homeostasis.

You might be wondering, what exactly is NSDR and Yoga Nidra? Well, it's a guided meditation technique that induces relaxation without falling asleep. The practice takes you through various stages of consciousness, promoting deep rest and rejuvenation of the mind and body. It's perfect for us in-between drinkers because we can do it anywhere, anytime, and even apps can guide you through it.

During the initial period of cutting back or stopping alcohol use, you may experience some sleep disturbances. Studies have shown that it can help reduce stress, anxiety, and even symptoms of depression. When we stop or reduce our alcohol intake, our brains may need time to adjust and find a new equilibrium. NSDR and Yoga Nidra can help support this process by allowing the mind to reset and recover. Practicing this technique gives your body the rest it needs, even if you're not sleeping a whole night. As we all know, adequate rest is vital for maintaining healthy habits and overall well-being. Now, let's talk about how to practice NSDR and Yoga Nidra. It's quite simple, and anyone can do it. Here's a basic breakdown:

1. Find a comfortable place to lie down or sit and remain undisturbed for about 20-30 minutes.
2. Close your eyes and take a few deep breaths, allowing your body and mind to settle.
3. Follow a guided NSDR or Yoga Nidra meditation from an app or a recorded session. The guidance will lead you through a series of

steps, such as body scanning, breath awareness, and visualization, all aimed at helping you achieve deep relaxation.

When the session ends, take your time to bring your awareness back to your surroundings gently. Open your eyes and slowly move your body, feeling refreshed and rejuvenated.

As in-between drinkers, we must have tools like NSDR and Yoga Nidra in our arsenal. It's helped me tremendously and can be done in as little as 10-20 minutes. It significantly improved my mental and physical well-being during the transition period. By incorporating this practice, we can help our minds and bodies find balance, making it much easier to maintain our newfound healthy relationship with alcohol. So, give it a try, and see for yourself the benefits of this powerful relaxation technique.

Overview:

- In-between drinkers' challenge: sleep disturbances
- Solution: Non-Sleep Deep Rest (NSDR) and Yoga Nidra
- Benefits: relaxation, reduced stress, and brain recovery
- Practice: guided meditation in a comfortable setting
- Duration: 10-20 minutes
- Importance: mental and physical balance during transition

Early Riser

"Early to bed and early to rise makes a man healthy, wealthy, and wise."

- BENJAMIN FRANKLIN.

There are three types of people regarding sleep patterns: owls, who thrive during late-night hours and rise later in the day; larks, early risers who naturally wake up at what some might consider a painfully early hour; and those who fall somewhere in between. For most of my early adult life, I considered myself an owl and later, somewhere in between. I believed anything before 6:00 AM was not for me, and I assumed being a lark wasn't in my DNA. However, I was wrong. With more distance between myself and alcohol, my body began to rise earlier and earlier on its own. Nowadays, my most creative time is when I write, and my body wakes up without an alarm clock between 4:00 and 5:00 AM.

I can tell you from experience that becoming an early riser is one of the most impactful decisions you can make for yourself. The early mornings are what I like to call "my time." Most people are still sleeping at this hour, and no one needs or asks for anything. The early hours are quiet, and your mind is fresh and unburdened from the previous day's busyness and stress. It's a great time to journal, meditate, create, and exercise. In the context of this book, the most significant benefit is the formation of a new habit: rising early.

The truth is, it's nearly impossible to be an early riser if you drink in the evenings. You'll also develop a newfound appreciation for mornings that will help you resist temptations at night. This time has become so precious that the thought of trading it for a fleeting pleasure followed by a tired, late start the next day is enough to curb cravings.

The value of early mornings became so significant in my life that whenever I experienced a thought or craving for alcohol, I was reminded that giving in would mean losing my precious morning time. This unexpected benefit of rising early reinforced my decision not to drink.

Even when tempted by "just one drink," I knew better. First, we know that "just one" is often a slippery slope and is unlikely to stop there. Second, I understood that even a single drink would disrupt my sleep enough to prevent me from waking up at 4 AM with a clear mind and a centered heart.

Becoming an early riser can benefit your mental health and wellness and reinforce your commitment to taking a break from alcohol. A great book called "The 5 AM Club" goes deeper into the benefits and strategies of becoming an early riser. I encourage you to check it out.

I'll leave you with this thought: Even if you can't envision yourself waking up as early as 4 or 5 AM and considering yourself an owl, I invite you to reconsider based on my experience. Our habits are not set in stone. You have the opportunity to decide or change that for yourself. I encourage you to try this life-changing practice for yourself. Embracing the early morning can transform your relationship with alcohol and help you establish healthier patterns for overall well-being.

Overview:

- There are three types of sleep patterns: owls, larks, and those in between.
- Becoming an early riser can be impactful for mental health and well-being.
- Early mornings offer quiet, creative, and productive time for personal growth.
- Early mornings can help resist temptations and curb cravings
- Habits are changeable, so consider early rising for personal transformation and healthier patterns.

Exercise Impulse

"Exercise is the key not only to physical health but to peace of mind."

- NELSON MANDELA.

Exercise profoundly impacts our mental well-being, including our ability to control impulses and establish new habits. In this chapter, we'll explore the benefits of exercise that go far beyond just physical health. Together, we'll uncover the neuroscience behind exercise and discuss how it can help us promote impulse control and habit formation.

The Science of Exercise
When we engage in physical activity, our brains undergo several changes contributing to improved mental health and cognitive function. Some of the essential mechanisms at work include neuroplasticity, neurogenesis, and the release of neurotransmitters.

Neuroplasticity: Exercise enhances neuroplasticity by stimulating the production of brain-derived neurotrophic factor (BDNF) protein. BDNF supports the neuron's growth, survival, and differentiation, allowing our brains to adapt and learn more effectively.

Neurogenesis: Research has shown that regular exercise, particularly aerobic exercise, can boost neurogenesis in the hippocampus, a region crucial for learning and memory. This increase in neuron production can positively effect on cognitive function and mood regulation.

Neurotransmitters: Exercise also increases the release of neuro-transmitters such as dopamine, serotonin, and norepinephrine. These chemicals are vital to regulating mood, motivation, and reward-seeking behavior and essential in impulse control and habit formation.

The Exercise Advantage: Impulse Control and New Habit Formation

Now let's explore how it can help us improve impulse control and facilitate the formation of new habits.

Elevated Mood and Motivation: The increased release of neurotransmitters during exercise enhances our mood and motivation. With better motivation and a more positive outlook, we're better equipped to resist impulsive decisions and focus on our long-term goals, such as taking a break from alcohol.

Sharper Cognitive Function: Exercise-induced neuroplasticity and neurogenesis improve cognitive function, including better executive functioning, attention, and memory. These cognitive improvements can enhance our ability to control impulses and make better decisions in challenging situations.

Habit Formation Through a Routine: Incorporating regular exercise into our daily routine can help us establish healthy habits. Sticking to a consistent exercise schedule trains our brains to expect and adapt to this new routine, making replacing old habits with new, healthier ones easier.

Stress Reduction: Exercise is a proven stress reliever. By reducing stress, we decrease the likelihood of resorting to unhealthy coping mechanisms, such as drinking alcohol, and instead focus on more constructive habits.

Increased Self-discipline: Regular exercise requires commitment and self-discipline. By cultivating these qualities, we strengthen our ability to resist impulsive behaviors and adhere to our goals, like taking a 66-day break from alcohol.

Choose an enjoyable activity to gain the power of exercise during your break, whether jogging, swimming, cycling, or weightlifting. You'll be more likely to stick to your exercise routine if it's something you genuinely look forward to.

Overview:

- Exercise benefits: Physical and mental well-being
- Neuroscience: Neuroplasticity, neurogenesis, neurotransmitters
- Exercise advantages: Mood elevation, motivation, cognitive function, habit formation, stress reduction, self-discipline
- Choose enjoyable activities using a consistent routine.

Meditation Control

"Meditation is the ultimate mobile device; you can use it anywhere, anytime, unobtrusively."

- SHARON SALZBERG.

Meditation, particularly mindfulness-based practices, has an impressive ability to enhance self-control. It achieves this by stimulating the prefrontal cortex, which governs executive functions such as decision-making, impulse management, and emotional regulation.

A groundbreaking study published in the International Journal of Neuropsychology revealed that with just 11 minutes of meditation, participants consumed less alcohol than the control group who didn't meditate (Karyadi et al., 2018). Meditation provides many benefits, but let's hone in on a few that are especially relevant in this context.

Stress Reduction
It's no secret that stress often drives us to alcohol. Meditation has been proven to help lower stress levels by regulating the body's stress response and promoting relaxation (Goyal et al., 2014). By managing stress more effectively, individuals are less likely to turn to alcohol as a coping mechanism.

Emotional Regulation
Meditation can enhance emotional regulation by increasing activity in brain regions linked to empathy, self-awareness, and emotional processing (Taren et al., 2015). Better emotional regulation can lead to an improved mood, reduced stress, and a heightened ability to resist cravings.

Neuroplasticity
Meditation promotes neuroplasticity, the brain's ability to adapt and change (Davidson & Lutz, 2008). By fostering neuroplasticity, meditation

can help reshape the neural pathways associated with alcohol dependence, ultimately supporting lasting habit change.

The combination of meditation's numerous advantages, such as improved self-control, reduced cravings, stress relief, enhanced emotional regulation, and increased neuroplasticity, all contribute to an environment that fosters successful habit change and recovery.

If you're anything like me and have struggled with meditation in the past, don't worry –plenty of fantastic resources and apps like *Calm* offer guided meditation. I've tried a few, and they make it simple and enjoyable to follow, requiring no more effort than finding a quiet spot and opening the app. So, give meditation a try and discover how it can powerfully support your journey.

Overview:

- Exercise benefits: Physical and mental well-being
- Neuroscience: Neuroplasticity, neurogenesis, neurotransmitters
- Exercise advantages: Mood elevation, motivation, cognitive function, habit formation, stress reduction, self-discipline
- Choose enjoyable activities: Consistent routine

Breathwork Mastery

"Through the art of breathwork, we tap into an ancient power, turning mere air into a healing force within."

- MIKE HARDENBROOK.

I believe everyone should do some form of breathwork, and I'd like to spend some time explaining with scientific evidence as to why: I began my breathwork journey in 2015, and it has been a game-changer for my mental well-being and overall happiness. With techniques like the Wim Hof method gaining traction, it's clear that more people are catching on to the power of intentional breath control.

The Wim Hof method involves three or more cycles of rapid, deep breathing followed by a breath-holding phase known as breath retention. Since performing the Wim Hof method, I've had breath holds for more than 5 minutes after exhaling! These long holds bring me into an altered state, and by the end, it's like I hit the reset button on those challenging days.

Before going further into this chapter, I'd like to mention that the Wim Hof method is only one option for breathwork. It's the method I can talk more about from personal experience. Some well-known alternatives are Pranayama, Holotropic Breathwork, Buteyko Method, Sudarshan Kriya (SKY), Transformational Breath, and 4-7-8 Breathing. I'm in the early stages of practicing Holotropic Breathwork and will write more after I have obtained greater experience with this method. Let's briefly cover some of the differences:

Wim Hof Method: Features controlled hyperventilation and breath retention, influencing the autonomic nervous system and immune response, known for increasing energy and stress resilience.

Holotropic Breathwork: Involves rapid breathing to stimulate emotional release and access deeper psychological states. It activates the sympathetic nervous system, often leading to emotional and personal insights.

Pranayama (Yogic Breathing): Comprises various techniques like alternate nostril breathing, focusing on breath regulation to balance energy, reduce stress and anxiety, and enhance focus.

Buteyko Breathing: Centers on nasal breathing and reduced breath volume to improve tissue oxygenation, beneficial for respiratory conditions like asthma.

Sudarshan Kriya (SKY): A rhythmic breathing practice shown to reduce stress, anxiety, and depression by influencing the body's levels of stress hormones and neurochemicals associated with well-being.

4-7-8 Breathing: A relaxation method involving a specific breathing pattern that calms the nervous system, useful for reducing anxiety and improving sleep.

Transformational Breath: Combines deep breathing with movement and sound for increased self-awareness and emotional release.

I have been talking about breathwork for several years, but what I've witnessed is most of the friends and colleagues who inquire about the benefits, do nothing with the advice. I've thought about why that is, and I think it's a combo of discomfort, discipline, and the unknown. I won't sugarcoat it – getting started with breathwork can be challenging and uncomfortable, as with anything new. However, I want to send a challenge to you directly to try it. The friends who did take action, have anecdotally reported a 100% positive and impactful experience.

I think I was originally drawn to Wim Hof when I heard a story on a podcast about how someone held their breath for several minutes. Ever since I was a kid, and to this day, I like to see how far I can swim in the pool from one side to the other. So, this drew me in for that reason, but that's not what has kept me practicing. Sure, being able to have long retention times is neat, but feeling like a million bucks after is the real benefit. You will have to experience it for yourself, but it takes you to a place of calm, a direct line to the parasympathetic nervous system, which I'll talk about shortly.

Here's a list of personal benefits I experience from breathwork: stress reduction, mood regulation, craving reduction, better cognition (less brain fog), increased mental and physical endurance, spiritually in-tune, and overall improved sense of well-being.

The benefits of breathwork are increasingly being validated by research. Let's break down some of the science. A study by Muzik et al. (2018) revealed that breathwork activates brain regions associated with self-control and emotional regulation. This supports our ability to replace old habits with new, healthier ones. The findings are not isolated; they form a growing body of evidence that underscores the impact breathwork has on the mind and body.

When we engage in rhythmic and deep breathing patterns, we're initiating a series of physiological changes. For example, rapid breathing leads to a decrease in carbon dioxide within the blood, causing a temporary rise in blood pH—a state known as respiratory alkalosis. This shift induces sensations of lightness and heightened awareness, which can be euphoric. In this case, we are literally getting high on our own supply!

The effects go beyond immediate sensations. Breathwork has been shown to interact with the autonomic nervous system, which is responsible for our fight-or-flight. Conversely, we activate the parasympathetic nervous system, which is the rest-and-digest response. By consciously manipulating our breathing, we can actually steer our body from a state of stress to one of calm. This empowers us, at almost any time, to achieve a state that can counteract the need for external stress relievers, such as alcohol.

Another study by Brown and Gerbarg (2005) on Sudarshan Kriya (SKY) highlighted its effectiveness in stress and emotional management. SKY, which uses rhythmic breathing patterns, differs from the Wim Hof method in both technique and effects. While the Wim Hof method involves a combination of controlled hyperventilation and breath retention, often combined with cold exposure, SKY focuses on cyclic, rhythmic patterns of breath. In terms of effects, the 2005 study indicates a reduction of stress, anxiety, and depression by lowering stress hormone levels and increasing neurochemicals like endorphins and serotonin. These results suggest a more direct influence on emotional regulation and mood enhancement compared to the Wim Hof method, which is more focused on enhancing physical resilience and stress response.

For me, breathwork has filled the meditation gap when traditional methods haven't quite hit the mark. As I mentioned, it's like hitting the reset button on life's stresses and worries. Plus, I've found that my breath retention times are a barometer for my mental and physical well-being. When I'm more stressed or sleep-deprived, my retention times take a nosedive, but when I'm in sync, they soar.

I'd like to stress that meditation is an incredible tool, one that I plan to immerse myself within. But at the time when I needed a mindful practice, it was not the tool for me. However, I still needed a way to tap into my parasympathetic nervous system. I remember one morning when I had to give a presentation to a large audience. I didn't sleep much, and my stress levels were at an all-time high; I opened a guided meditation app hoping to bring myself back down to a manageable level but found my mind wandered incessantly, and I struggled to achieve any sense of calm I was seeking. However, when I switched to a breathwork session, focusing on the rhythm and depth of my breaths, I felt more engaged. The physical act of inhaling deeply, holding, and then exhaling required enough concentration to keep my mind from wandering. This active engagement provided a sense of focus that allowed me to unplug from my stream of active thoughts. After the session, I noticed a measurable improvement in my mood and confidence. Despite not sleeping well, my energy and clarity were restored to more normal levels. I was able to get on stage and present that day with confidence.

I was convinced breathwork was (one) of the mindful practices I would regularly incorporate into my life. However, as I prepared to write this book, I needed to give more thought as to why I connected with breathwork over other practices. The conclusion I came to; breathwork offers a more active approach. Where traditional meditation emphasizes stillness and mental focus, breathwork involves dynamic breathing patterns that influence my physiological and mental state. This active engagement helps me feel more in control and aware of my body's responses. The immediate physical feedback – like the increase in heart rate and focus to slow it down – provides tangible feedback that I struggled with in traditional meditation. Another aspect, as an athlete, is my ability to measure progress through breath retention times gives me a quantifiable attribute to my practice. I don't make it about a competition on retention times with others, nor myself even, but I find it easier to track where I am mentally and physically at that moment. I want to offer this as an alternative to those who struggle with meditation since that's been my experience. I think these practices also come in different phases of our lives for a reason when we need them most. I could very well see myself in another phase putting more emphasis on meditation. It's my goal to provide options with methods of mindfulness and stress management that connect with where you are, at this moment.

If you are considering starting breathwork, I'd pick one from the list above and do a search for some guided videos. There are plenty of great and free resources to give it a try at home. The free and paid versions of the Wim Hof app are easy to use and inexpensive. Remember it can be challenging at first, the key is consistency and openness to the experience.

Breathwork is a pathway to better understanding ourselves and managing life's ups and downs. It has the potential to be truly transformative – I know it has been for me. I urge you to give it a try.

Overview:

- Breathwork involves deep breathing and breath retention.
- Benefits: stress reduction, emotional regulation, curbing cravings, improved cognitive function
- Breathwork activates brain regions for self-control and emotional regulation.
- Breath retention times indicate mental and physical well-being.
- Challenging but potentially transformative

PART

06

Alternative Approaches

*"If you want something you've never had, you must be
willing to do something you've never done."*

- THOMAS JEFFERSON.

Psychedelics

Disclaimer: In many regions, psychedelics are considered illegal, and
their possession, sale, or use can lead to legal consequences. This chapter
is intended for educational purposes and does not encourage or endorse
any illegal activities.

This chapter may not be for everyone, and I know that. The treatment
outcomes in this chapter vary based on several factors related to your
alcohol use; quantity, frequency, duration, as well as the underlying
reasons for drinking. Your interest in psychedelics may not even be related
to alcohol. The aim here is to provide the information necessary to
understand the benefits and risks of psychedelic-assisted therapies. It's
about feeling drawn to this path for your own reasons, not because you
were swayed by persuasive arguments. In the pages that follow, you'll
discover both statistical evidence and personal narratives that suggest

psychedelics could be more effective in treating alcohol dependence than any treatments currently approved by the FDA.

At the time of this writing, we find ourselves amid a "psychedelic renaissance," a significant shift after decades of regulatory and societal restrictions that began in the 1970s. Many are unaware that the study of psychedelics for treating various mental disorders began in the 1950s, yielding some impressive patient outcomes. Unfortunately, this work was put to a stop by legislation and pushed into the underground for forty years. Now, with the support of organizations like MAPS, the Multidisciplinary Association for Psychedelic Studies, we're seeing a breakthrough in both the legalization and public perception. The shift is reopening critical work for individuals struggling with substance abuse disorders, PTSD, depression, anxiety, and trauma. We stand at the threshold of a transformative era in mental health care.

Psychedelics vs Psychedelic-Assisted Therapy

I think it's important to make a clear distinction between using psychedelics and psychedelic-assisted therapy. While these medicines present incredible opportunities to treat chronic illness, they are not a magic pill. When we are talking about psychedelics in this chapter, I am not referring to getting a bag of mushrooms from your brother's old college roommate and seeing what happens. When I share my work with MDMA, the common response I will get is, "Oh, I've done ecstasy in college" or, "I did molly when I went to a concert." I usually try to respond with a note of positivity, but these experiences are like comparing apples to oranges. I also did MDMA and Psilocybin in college, and I can tell you that while the medicines may be the same (depending on purity) the experience and outcomes are far from the same.

When I am referring to psychedelics here, I am talking about the use under guided supervision, in a controlled environment, in conjunction with ongoing integration work. The combination of integration and psychedelics is where the magic can lead to transformation. The word "magic" is not hyperbole, because unlike other medicines that tend to mask symptoms, psychedelics indicate a long-term cure to chronic mental illness. The term integration work is not universally understood, and why should it be, it's not a mainstream term. Let's explore together further in-depth what it is that makes the psychedelic road so much different than any other approach to mental illness.

When we engage in psychedelic integration, it's important to understand that it involves more than just reflecting on our experiences. This process allows us to make sense of what we've encountered, particularly when dealing with complex emotional content. Psychedelic experiences can bring up deep-seated memories and insights, and integration is the key to incorporating all of this into our everyday lives.

Integration is a continuous journey of self-discovery and growth. It's not limited to a single event but it's an ongoing process where the experience furthers our personal development. Incorporating practices like meditation or mindfulness helps us stay connected to the knowledge from our psychedelic session. The ultimate goal of psychedelic integration is to turn the session into lasting change in how we understand ourselves, interact with others, and live our lives.

Early Studies:
Acknowledgment: I want to extend my thanks to Dr. Rayyan Zafar of Imperial College London for his invaluable insights on psychedelic research for AUD. His permission to use elements of his work has significantly enriched this chapter, deepening our understanding of the subject.

Let's talk about the history of Bill Wilson, a history that may surprise you. Wilson was the founder of Alcoholics Anonymous, and authored "Distilled Spirits," reflecting on his alcoholism journey. In 1934, he received treatment at New York State Hospital with various alkaloids and plants like belladonna and henbane, which are not typical deliriants.

This treatment induced an altered state of consciousness in Wilson, marking his first break from alcohol cravings and the cycle of withdrawal. This shift in consciousness, which changed his obsessive thoughts about addiction, was a turning point. As a result, Wilson persuaded the NIH in the U.S. to fund LSD research trials. In these trials, conducted during the 1950s and 60s, over 500 patients received a high dose of LSD.

The trial divided participants into two groups: 250 received a placebo, and 250 received LSD. The data showed an effect size of 2, indicating that those treated with LSD were twice as likely to reduce heavy drinking days compared to the placebo group, 60% of the LSD group showed improvement, compared to 38% in the placebo group. Medical statistics use something called the "number needed to treat," metric to gauge an intervention's effectiveness. In comparison to current alcohol use disorder treatments like nalmethine and acamprosate, which require treating 20 patients for one to recover, all LSD's number needed to treat was merely six.

This indicates that LSD is two to three times more effective than existing pharmacological treatments. A single high dose led to sustained reductions in alcohol misuse for up to six months and up to three months of abstinence. This highlights the potency of a single 12-hour treatment for individuals who have struggled with alcohol addiction for decades, marking an early phase of such research.

In the late 1970s and early 1980s, MDMA emerged as a novel psychotherapeutic tool. While these were primarily used in relation to addressing PTSD, it's worth noting that PTSD and alcohol use can be linked. The medicine has a unique ability to create feelings of empathy, openness, and reduced fear. These early explorations laid the groundwork for its later use in treating conditions such as Post-Traumatic Stress Disorder (PTSD).

The use of MDMA in these therapeutic sessions was characterized by an increased sense of emotional connectivity between the therapist and patient. This facilitated a more profound therapeutic engagement, where patients could confront and process traumatic experiences in a supportive and emotionally open setting. Despite the lack of formal clinical trials, anecdotal reports from therapists suggested promising results where conventional therapy had limited success.

Unfortunately, the recreational use of MDMA or "Ecstasy" at the time led to increased legal pressure. In 1985, MDMA was classified as a Schedule I substance in the United States, effectively halting its legal use in therapy. This prohibition marked the end of this early exploratory phase of MDMA in psychotherapy.

Recent Studies:

In 2015, the first modern clinical trial using psilocybin to treat alcohol abuse disorder was conducted. Participants received two high doses, spaced four weeks apart. This open-label trial focused on comparing pre- and post-treatment scores.

Results showed a significant decrease in drinking days, from about 45% to 10%, within four weeks, a trend that continued for up to 25 to 36 weeks (approximately six months). A notable finding was the reduction in craving scores, a crucial indicator of relapse risk. Initially, participants had an average craving score of 16 out of 20. The score dropped by 50% to 8 by week 36 after two sessions.

The study sought to understand the underlying reasons for these changes. One approach involved the Mystical Experience Questionnaire, assessing participants' experiences during their psilocybin sessions, including feelings of oneness, ego dissolution, and tranquility. The results indicated a correlation between the intensity of the mystical experience and a decrease in heavy drinking days. Higher mystical experience scores were linked to greater long-term reductions in alcohol consumption.

The strength of this correlation was significant, with those scoring highest on the Mystical Experience Questionnaire showing a 60% reduction in drinking days. This suggests the profound impact of the psychedelic experience itself on treatment outcomes.

A larger phase-two clinical trial at New York University found psilocybin to be twice as effective as a placebo in reducing heavy drinking days. This trial confirmed the lasting effects observed in the initial study, with a clear distinction between the placebo group and those receiving psilocybin treatment.

We now turn to the research on the effectiveness of MDMA and alcohol. Participants in the study consumed on average 130 units of alcohol weekly, equivalent to 15 bottles of wine or 5 liters of vodka. These individuals underwent detoxification before the trial, which involved three sessions of MDMA-assisted psychotherapy, incorporating elements of the MAPS protocol and motivational enhancement therapy (MET).

Significant results were observed, with participants reducing their alcohol consumption from 130 units per week to approximately 18.7 units nine months post-detox. A substantial decrease in heavy drinking. The study also addressed concerns about the potential mood-lowering effects of MDMA, commonly referred to as "comedowns" or "Blue Tuesdays." The research aimed to ensure that MDMA did not lead to depression in patients. Interestingly, the data showed an improvement in mood following MDMA administration, contradicting the belief that MDMA inevitably leads to a mood decline.

The study emphasizes the importance of context in drug use, suggesting that negative effects like comedowns are more associated with the environment of drug use (such as nightclubs and mixing substances) rather than the pharmacology of MDMA itself. This distinction between the clinical and recreational use of MDMA is highlighted, pointing out the crucial role of psychotherapeutic elements in MDMA therapy, which involves active trauma-based therapeutic engagement. This approach differs significantly from therapies involving psilocybin, which is more focused on an internal journey with therapeutic guidance provided mainly before and after the psychedelic experience.

Currently, there is significant interest in the therapeutic potential of drugs like ketamine, especially in the context of a phase 2 study conducted by Awaken, a UK-based company. This study combined ketamine with psychotherapy, demonstrating a mean abstinence rate of 86%. In contrast, the group that received a placebo and psychoeducation showed about a 70% abstinence rate. While the difference of 15% may not seem substantial, it is statistically significant. Compared to other clinical trials where a notable number of individuals do not respond to treatments, Ketamine emerges as one of the most effective and legally available psychedelic therapies at present.

Ketamine
Benefits: Reduces cravings, promotes introspection, and facilitates new perspectives on addiction.
Science: As an NMDA receptor antagonist, Ketamine promotes neuroplasticity and disrupts maladaptive thought patterns. It also offers rapid antidepressant effects.

Psilocybin
Benefits: Induces profound mystical experiences, increased self-awareness, and enhanced emotional processing.

Science: Psilocybin targets serotonin 2A receptors (5-HT2A), alters perception and cognition, facilitates introspection, and can help "reset" the brain's default mode network (DMN).

MDMA
Benefits: Increases empathy and compassion, addressing emotional and interpersonal addiction-related issues.
Science: MDMA boosts serotonin, dopamine, and norepinephrine, promoting feelings of closeness, trust, and emotional openness, helping individuals process unresolved emotions and traumas.

DMT
Benefits: Induces intense, immersive experiences for personal insights and shifts in perspective.
Science: DMT acts on 5-HT2A receptors, like psilocybin, helping individuals confront their addiction and gain transformative insights.

5-MeO-DMT
Benefits: Induces deeply spiritual and mystical experiences, promoting personal growth and reevaluation of alcohol use.
Science: 5-MeO-DMT acts on 5-HT2A receptors and leads to shifts in values, priorities, and perspectives, allowing individuals to address the root cause of their addiction and make lasting changes in their behavior.

Microdosing
Benefits: Taking sub-perceptual doses of psychedelics (e.g., LSD or psilocybin) can enhance mood, cognition, and creativity without causing intense hallucinogenic experiences. This practice may help individuals develop healthier coping mechanisms and improve overall mental well-being, contributing to reduced alcohol consumption.
Science: The exact mechanisms of microdosing are not fully understood. Microdosing is believed to modulate the brain's serotonin system, improving mood, focus, and emotional resilience. These factors can support individuals in addressing underlying issues driving their addiction and developing healthier habits.

Personal Experience

The saying, "If you want something you've never had, you must be willing to do something you've never done," has been a guiding principle in my life. I've shifted between being an observer and actively participating in my journey, consistently striving for growth and transformation.

In my younger days, I experimented in a recreational sense with psychedelics. However, those experiences have no comparison to my intentional and guided work with these medicines. I'd like to share some of those experiences, as well as the insights and results gained in my life. I'd like to note that the experiences below were spread out over the course of a five-year period. Between my work with medicine, I dedicated a great deal of time to research and integration.

Finding the Spirit Within

I wanted to go down this exploration into the unknown parts of my psyche, I was drawn to it on my own accord. However, despite over a year of research, reading studies, and watching documentaries, I still had limited knowledge and no actual experience. This is in part a motivator here for me to overshare on this experience. So, if you are considering psychedelics, you can learn from both statistical evidence and anecdotal stories. Please know that my experiences are unique to me, and others may and likely will report them as different.

Through a series of friends, I was connected to what is referred to as a facilitator, or guide, that works with these medicines. I had an interest in the Ayahuasca experience. I didn't have the depth of knowledge to know what would be the right path, but I knew I wanted a profound, life-changing experience. I was offered the opportunity to do a session with 5-MeO-DMT, known as Bufo or Toad. This was not Ayahuasca, although the naming has similarities N, N-Dimethyltryptamine, or DMT. They both invoke a mystical experience but with some key differences. The 5-MEO experience is fast-acting, fast to metabolize (wear off), and a much stronger journey. The entire journey lasts about 15-30 minutes. Although it's short, there is no concept of time in that space. It could feel like minutes, hours, days, weeks, months, it really depends on the journey.

The subsequent journey is challenging to put into words, and even harder not to sound a little crazy while doing it. It's a little like a caveman stepping into a time machine, then coming back and explaining to other cavemen, with a limited vocabulary, what was seen. But here I go, hopefully sounding better than a caveman. The initial onset is very rapid, I was trying to make sense of it all. All senses and reality began to distort, with a sensation of rapid velocity. As it became more challenging, I reminded myself to trust, surrender, and let go. Once I did that, I emerged into a space of what I would describe as pure bliss and love. No cognitive thoughts, no longer identifying as "Mike, who grew up in Arizona, married with three kids." Instead, it was a knowledge of existence. A sense of connectivity to everything that is, and ever was. It was a knowing, without thought, without a divided sense of self. I felt as if I had met my true self, essence, or subconscious, for the first time.

What I experienced was ego death, a disintegration of the self, and emerged with newfound insights into my existence. I had begun my journey to this medicine with the hopes of unrooting my issues in life, anxiety, and issues with alcohol. However, what I emerged with was something completely different. All my life I have wanted to believe in God, but was never fully able to believe with true faith. I just had too many questions and doubts. This experience unequivocally changed that forever, I felt God. There is a saying, "The medicine will show you exactly what you need to know." That day, which continues to this day, forever changed my spiritual connection and belief.

I also noticed a loss of interest in alcohol in the subsequent days, weeks, and then months. The allure diminished, while my faith grew. Looking back, what I didn't do enough of to get the most from that experience was integration. While I would journal and ponder that experience, I didn't know how to process all the messages that were received and put them into greater action. For this reason, I emphasize the importance of integration. It's often overlooked in value for those who start out, as the medicine is more appealing and newer.

Though 5-MEO-DMT was transformative for me, I recognize it might not be the best starting point for everyone. Particularly in regard to alcohol. While it offers deep spiritual insights and aids neuroplasticity and neurogenesis, it's not universally palatable.

Opening My Heart

My experience with 5-MEO was transformational for my spirituality, but I still felt there must be something left to explore in my "real life." I had questions; did I have trauma I was unaware of? Was there something I needed to explore related to the self-sabotaging habit I was repeating? This led me to be offered a chance to work with therapy-assisted MDMA.

Before I share my experience, I'd like to explain what a typical session with this medicine looks like. Most people who have taken MDMA will be surprised by the dramatic difference in the experience in this format. What is unique to this medicine, is how the set and setting will change the effects. In a recreational setting, the effects are also euphoric, feelings of love and empathy are enhanced. However, when you introduce a calm setting, set your intentions, and use things like eye coverings and strategic music related to your emotions, the experience is enhanced. You go very internal, and the intensity can be modulated. I find with my eyes covered, and I am settled into the music, that the intensity can be an eight or nine out of ten. In this state, I have vivid visions, which are very psychedelic in nature. However, if I find them to be too intense, I can remove the eye coverings, sit up, and interact with my guide, the intensity can then be lowered to a two or three on the scale. This allows me to go in and out as needed, and process specific experiences as they come to me.

In my first session, I set the intention to find the root of my self-sabotaging behaviors. The effects came on gently, I found my mind in an almost daydream-like state of drifting in my thoughts and mind. I found myself observing my now wife, Priscilla. She was in a celestial form, floating with her long curly hair as an extension of her power. This drew me into a long contemplation about our relationship. We had been together for fourteen years, and had three children together, but were on a path to separation at that time. The medicine allowed me to connect new pathways and observations around our relationship. What I realized was that I was 99.99% fully committed, but because I had my own issues with the contract of marriage, that .01% was causing the major problems in our relationship to continue to grow. I was able to view our relationship through her perspective and understand with empathy, instead of defensiveness. After that one session of MDMA, our relationship took a 180-degree turn. We no longer fought; we began to grow as a couple again. We had a deeper love and respect than ever before. Shortly after, we were engaged, had a beautiful celebration of our love, and are now happily married. I attribute this session to saving my relationship and providing a loving home for my three children to grow up in, with happily married parents. This marked the moment where I saw these medicines as not only life-changing but world-changing. That session not only changed the lives of Priscilla and I, but also our children, and their children, and so on.

Flying Past Fears
About a year after my MDMA experience, I found myself wanting to continue that work. However, it was inaccessible to me at the time. Ketamine, which is legal, appeared like it could be the next best thing in my mind. I thought of it as a milder medicine I could try. However, I was incorrect in thinking it was milder; it was just different.

You have to be mindful when choosing a Ketamine clinic. The background of those running them, including their bedside manner, will impact the experience. I was aware of this in my research. Some offices have a gurney approach, that's to say, they wheel patients in and out as fast as possible. It's the white fluorescent lights, white lab coat, and treated like any other medical procedure. This was not the type of experience I was looking for. I was able to find an office in Scottsdale that had a wonderful bedside manner, the office walls were decorated in murals, and the rooms had cosmic lighting and essential oils.

The Ketamine is administered through an IV as an infusion and lasts about an hour. I was in a reclined chair, given eye coverings and music designed for the experience. One thing that I have noticed when it comes to Ketamine, is that people have very distinct reactions, some have mild meditative-like experiences, while others may have profound psychedelic experiences. I am the latter in this case. The medicine came on rather slowly, but I soon found myself in a space that looked much like the multiverse in a Marvel movie. I was floating in the universe with stars, exploding neon colors, flying like Superman between outer space, walking through ancient temples, space and time folding, but I still had this fear lingering. At one point I found myself wrapped in a cotton candy-like cloud. It was soothing, calm, and I felt safe. However, I could see off into the distance at one point, something difficult that I needed to address. I didn't want to, I wanted to stay comfortable. Eventually, though, I couldn't avoid it being there. Like Superman, I decided to fly at it straight on. But what happened was a surprise, it blew right past me. It told me that I didn't need to take problems on directly all of the time, and when that happened all of my fears evaporated. I then settled into the medicine even further with this thought, "Take me as far as we can go."

I was able to be the observer without fear, judgment, or difficulty. I could physically feel new connections and pathways in my mind forming. Even the feeling that negative ones were being removed. There was less cognitive processing, and more of a "knowing" throughout the session. After the session, I took plenty of time to rest and sit with my thoughts. A noticeable sensation I had was this feeling that I was in a plastic state with my mind and habits; like that fresh coat of snow I had mentioned before. One of the problems that I was dealing with, was ruminating thoughts about my health and death. I had a few medical issues recently, and it had taken over my everyday thoughts. However, before the treatment, I took a long test assessment for PTSD symptoms, which can happen for a variety of reasons. Not all PTSD is related to trauma with a capital T, it can develop and grow from smaller traumas. To my surprise, I was showing symptoms of PTSD.

In the days and months to follow, I experienced an increase in mood and confidence and a decrease in general anxiety. More specifically, my ruminating thoughts over my health had completely gone away. A month after my session, I took the same PTSD test again. My improvement down to the exact percentage, was 100% improvement. I found that fitting because that's exactly how I felt, 100% better.

Caution and Proper Guidance

It's crucial to emphasize that using psychedelics to address habits and alcohol should be done under the guidance of trained professionals, in controlled therapeutic settings. While the benefits can be significant, these substances also carry potential risks and should be approached with caution and proper supervision.

Educate Yourself and Go Deeper

For those interested in psychedelic research, the Multidisciplinary Association for Psychedelic Studies (MAPS) is a primary resource. Established by Rick Doblin, MAPS focuses on the research and development of medical, legal, and cultural contexts for people to benefit from the careful use of psychedelics. Their website, https://maps.org, offers access to a range of studies, publications, and updates in this field.

Another significant resource is the work of Dr. Rick Strassman. His book, "The Psychedelic Handbook," provides an in-depth look at psychedelic research. Dr. Strassman's contributions over the last 30 years have been influential in the study of psychedelic substances. His insights on topics like neuroplasticity and neurogenesis are valuable for understanding the potential future directions of psychedelic research.

Summary

Four key areas have been identified as affected by psychedelic treatment: increased connectedness and acceptance decreased negative cognitive biases, reduced rumination and thought suppression, and increased openness. These factors are crucial in overcoming various dependence and mental health issues.

We are still in the early phases of the renaissance of psychedelics. It is my goal to share both clinical studies, backed by science, and anecdotal evidence of my own personal experience.

The power of psychedelics to redefine your relationship with alcohol is an exciting and evolving area of research. With proper guidance and a commitment to self-discovery, you may find that these medicines can play a pivotal role in redefining your relationship with alcohol.

Overview:

- Psychedelics gaining attention for potential therapeutic benefits
- Addressing mental health disorders and addiction
- Studies showing significant impact on problematic drinking
- Psychedelics promote neuroplasticity and facilitate brain changes
- Overview of various psychedelics
- Microdosing: Enhances mood, cognition, and creativity
- Use psychedelics under trained professionals' guidance in controlled settings
- Educate yourself and explore the potential of psychedelics for personal growth and habit transformation

Cannabis Debate

*"Moderation is the balance between two extremes, the
excess and the deficiency."*

- ARISTOTLE.

You might be wondering if using cannabis during your 66-day alcohol break is a feasible option. In this chapter, we'll weigh the pros and cons of incorporating cannabis into your break from alcohol, emphasizing the significance of proceeding with caution to avoid replacing one unhealthy habit with another. Keep in mind our ultimate goal is to cultivate a healthier, more balanced lifestyle that improves our overall well-being.

The Neuroscience of Cannabis
Cannabis impacts the brain by interacting with the endocannabinoid system, a crucial player in regulating various physiological processes, such as mood, memory, and appetite. The primary psychoactive compound in cannabis, delta-9-tetrahydrocannabinol (THC), binds to cannabinoid receptors in the brain, resulting in the familiar effects of relaxation, euphoria, and heightened sensory perception.

The Pros of Cannabis

Diminished Alcohol Cravings: Cannabis can help alleviate alcohol cravings, making it simpler to abstain from drinking during the 66-day break.

Alternative Relaxation Method: For those of us who consume alcohol to unwind, cannabis offers a different avenue for relaxation and stress relief without the harmful effects associated with excessive alcohol consumption.

Potential Medical Benefits: Cannabis has demonstrated relief for various conditions, including anxiety and insomnia. If you're using cannabis for therapeutic purposes, it may be beneficial during your alcohol break.

The Cons of Cannabis

Risk of Substitution: The primary concern with using cannabis during the alcohol break is the potential to replace one unhealthy habit with another. It's vital to remain mindful of your cannabis consumption and ensure it doesn't become a new dependency.

Hinder Personal Growth: While cannabis can provide relaxation and stress relief, it may also impair cognitive function, memory, and reaction time. These effects could hinder your ability to fully immerse yourself in the introspective and personal growth aspects of the 66-day alcohol break.

If you decide to incorporate cannabis, follow these guidelines:

Be Mindful of Your Intentions: Use cannabis with a clear purpose, such as relaxation or pain relief, rather than as a substitute for alcohol.

opt for Low-THC Strains or CBD Products: Low-THC cannabis strains or CBD (cannabidiol) products can offer relaxation and stress relief without the intense psychoactive effects associated with high-THC strains.

Practice Moderation: Avoid excessive consumption, which could lead to negative consequences like dependency or impaired cognitive function.

Monitor Your Progress: Keep track of your cannabis use and its impact on your alcohol break journey. If you notice any negative patterns emerging, reconsider your cannabis consumption.

Remember, the key to success is being honest with yourself and staying committed to your personal growth and transformation journey.

Overview:

- Cannabis during 66-day alcohol break
- Pros: diminished alcohol cravings, alternative relaxation method, potential medical benefits
- Cons: risk of substitution, hindering personal growth
- Guidelines: be mindful of intentions, opt for low-THC strains or CBD products, practice moderation, monitor progress

EMDR Therapy

"The only way out is through."

- ROBERT FROST.

EMDR works by helping the brain reprocess distressing memories or emotions, which can be the root cause of many unwanted habits. It involves bilateral stimulation, such as eye movements, tapping, or sounds, to activate both brain hemispheres. This bilateral stimulation helps the brain reprocess traumatic or distressing memories and integrate them into our cognitive framework.

But why does this matter when we're talking about habits? Well, sometimes, our habits are driven by unresolved emotions or experiences. By helping the brain reprocess these memories, EMDR can essentially "rewire" our brain, making it easier to let go of habits that no longer serve us.

The success rates of EMDR are pretty impressive. Multiple studies have shown that EMDR effectively treats a variety of issues, including trauma, anxiety, and depression (Shapiro, 2014). While specific research on EMDR for alcohol-related habits might be limited, the overall effectiveness of EMDR in addressing underlying emotional issues suggests that it could be a valuable tool for those looking to change their relationship with alcohol.

So, what can you expect if you decide to give EMDR a try? The process usually starts with a trained therapist guiding you through eye movements or other forms of bilateral stimulation while you recall distressing memories or emotions. Over time, you may notice that these memories or emotions become less intense, and you'll start feeling more in control of your habits.

One example of a positive outcome from EMDR therapy might be someone who used to reach for a drink every time they felt stressed. After a few sessions of EMDR, they might find that the urge to drink in response to stress has significantly diminished, allowing them to explore healthier coping mechanisms instead.

Now, you might be wondering if you can do EMDR at home or if you need to visit a professional. While some self-help resources and apps are available for EMDR, I highly recommend working with a trained EMDR therapist, at least initially. They can guide you through the process safely and effectively, ensuring you get the most out of your EMDR experience.

Overview:

- EMDR helps reprocess distressing memories or emotions
- Bilateral stimulation activates both brain hemispheres
- Unresolved emotions or experiences can drive habits
- EMDR has impressive success rates for various issues
- The process involves a trained therapist guiding through eye movements or bilateral stimulation
- EMDR can reduce the intensity of memories or emotions and improve habit control
- Working with a trained EMDR therapist is recommended over self-help resources

TMS Treatment

*"We cannot solve our problems with the same thinking we
used when we created them."*

- ALBERT EINSTEIN.

Let's discuss synaptic plasticity and a relatively unknown therapy called
Transcranial Magnetic Stimulation (TMS). Our brain has billions of
neurons that communicate with each other through connections called
synapses. Synaptic plasticity is the brain's ability to reorganize these
connections, which allows us to learn new things and adapt to our
environment.

TMS is a non-invasive therapy that uses magnetic fields to stimulate
specific brain areas. By targeting these areas, TMS can help strengthen or
weaken synaptic connections, promoting synaptic plasticity and making it
easier for us to break unwanted habits.

You might wonder how successful TMS is for people looking to take
a break from alcohol. While most studies on TMS have focused on
depression and other mental health issues, emerging evidence suggests that
it also could be effective in changing alcohol-related habits (Herremans et
al., 2018). More research is needed, but the initial findings are promising,
and TMS could be a game-changer for many people seeking to transform
their relationship with alcohol.

So, what does TMS treatment look like? During a TMS session, you'll
be seated comfortably in a chair while a trained professional places a
magnetic coil near your head. The coil sends targeted magnetic pulses to
specific areas of your brain involved in habit formation. Most TMS
sessions last about 20-40 minutes, and you'll typically need multiple
sessions over several weeks to experience the full benefits.

One of the great things about TMS is that it can be personalized to your
needs. Your TMS practitioner can adjust the treatment to stimulate the
most relevant brain regions based on your goals and the habits you'd like
to change.

As for the cost, TMS can be somewhat pricey, with sessions often ranging from $200 to $500 each. However, some insurance companies may cover the treatment, so it's worth checking with your provider. Investing in your well-being is invaluable, and TMS could be a powerful tool to help you transform your habits.

Synaptic plasticity and TMS offer an innovative, science-backed approach to changing our relationship with alcohol. By harnessing the brain's ability to reorganize itself, TMS may help us break unwanted habits and build healthier ones in their place.

Overview:

- Synaptic plasticity: the brain's ability to reorganize connections.
- Transcranial Magnetic Stimulation (TMS) promotes synaptic plasticity.
- TMS is primarily studied for depression and mental health issues.
- Emerging evidence suggests TMS effectiveness in changing alcohol-related habits.
- TMS treatment involves targeted magnetic pulses to brain areas involved in habit formation.
- Personalized TMS treatments can be adjusted based on individual goals.
- The cost of TMS sessions can be high, but some insurance companies may cover it.
- TMS offers an innovative, science-backed approach to changing your relationship with alcohol.

Virtual Reality

"The best way to predict the future is to invent it."

- ALAN KAY.

Technological advancements have recently brought virtual reality (VR) for cue exposure therapy. Cue exposure is a form of treatment that exposes you to stimuli or "cues" that trigger your desire to drink, to reduce the power these cues hold over you. By repeatedly facing these cues in a controlled environment, you can learn to manage your cravings and better resist the temptation to drink.

Several studies have explored the potential of VR in aiding cue exposure therapy. A 2019 study by Son et al. found that VR-based cue exposure therapy effectively reduced alcohol cravings in participants, suggesting that VR can be a valuable tool for taking a break from alcohol.

One of the benefits of VR is that it allows for immersive, customizable experiences. You can tailor your virtual environment to include specific triggers that you find challenging. VR can also be used at home, making it a more accessible option.

Companies like Limbix and Psious are working on creating VR experiences specifically designed for mental health and addiction treatment. While these technologies are still in their early stages, they hold promise for the future of cue exposure therapy.

Aside from cue exposure, VR also enhances your meditation and mindfulness practices. If you explore the world of VR, apps like *Calm, Headspace,* or *Guided Meditation VR* can provide you with an immersive meditation experience. By immersing yourself in calming, virtual environments, you can potentially deepen your experience.

Keep in mind that VR technologies for cue exposure and meditation are still relatively new, so more resources and options will likely emerge.

Overview:

- Studies show that VR-based cue exposure therapy effectively reduces cravings.
- VR allows for immersive, customizable experiences tailored to personal triggers.
- Companies like Limbix and Psious are developing VR for mental health and addiction treatment.
- *Calm, Headspace,* and *Guided Meditation* VR are immersive meditation apps.
- VR technologies are still relatively new, with more resources likely to emerge in the future.

PART

07

Future Planning

"The first step toward change is awareness. The second step is acceptance."

- NATHANIEL BRANDEN.

Self-Evaluation

You've taken a huge step towards reshaping your relationship with alcohol and unlocking a life full of joy and success. Now, it's time to take a moment for self-evaluation, to look back at the journey you've embarked on, and to assess the changes you've made. You can keep moving forward with renewed enthusiasm and confidence by recognizing the sacrifices your old habits cost you and appreciating your gains in your quest for a healthier life. So, let's dive in and reflect on this incredible transformation.

First, let's examine the costs of your old habits. Before you embarked on this 66-day break, your relationship with alcohol may have led to various negative consequences. Consider the following areas of your life and reflect on how your old habits may have impacted them:

Relationships: Did alcohol strain your connections with family, friends, or romantic partners? Were there misunderstandings or conflicts that arose as a result of your drinking?

Health: Did alcohol consumption lead to physical or mental health issues such as sleep disturbances, weight gain, or mood swings?

Career: Did your performance at work suffer due to your drinking habits? Were you less productive, motivated, or focused?

Personal growth: Did alcohol keep you from pursuing your passions or interests? Were you less likely to engage in activities that brought you joy, personal fulfillment, or self-improvement?

Let's focus on the positive changes you've experienced during your 66-day break. Reflect on the following areas and think about the progress you've made:

Relationships: Have your relationships with loved ones deepened since reducing alcohol consumption? Have you been able to communicate more effectively and foster stronger bonds with the people who matter most to you?

Health: Have you noticed a boost in your overall well-being, both physically and mentally? Are you enjoying better sleep, increased energy levels, and a more stable mood?

Career: Has your work life improved due to your newfound clarity and focus? Have you been able to take on new challenges, exceed expectations, and find greater satisfaction in your professional life?

Personal growth: Have you discovered new passions, interests, or hobbies that fill you with joy and purpose? Can you now devote more time and energy to activities that contribute to your personal development and happiness?

Spirituality: Has your journey led to a deeper connection with your spiritual self? Have you found new meaning, purpose, or inner peace while moving away from alcohol?

By reflecting on these questions, you can better understand the actual impact alcohol has had on your life and how your 66-day break has empowered you to make positive changes in various aspects of your life.

Overview:

- Assess the costs of old habits in relationships, health, career, and personal growth.
- Reflect on positive changes in relationships, health, career, personal growth, and spirituality with an alcohol break.
- Recognize sacrifices and appreciate gains for a healthier life
- Renewed enthusiasm and confidence for continued transformation
- Develop a clearer understanding of alcohol's impact and empowerment from the break

Forgetful Mind

"To change ourselves effectively, we first have to change
our perceptions."

- STEPHEN COVEY.

You may have stopped drinking because you want to go from good to great, or maybe you quit because your drinking has become too uncomfortable. In either case, after going without alcohol, you will move into your new normal. When this happens, it is common for many people to forget what drove them to make the change in the first place. A typical scenario usually occurs after 30 to 60 days and even more commonly at 90 to 180 days. You feel great, your mind is clear, and your sleep is better than ever. Everything seems to be going well in your life, but occasionally you might think, "Maybe I'll just have a couple of drinks just one night," or "Maybe a sangria on the beach during vacation might be a nice treat."

What is going on in your mind during these times is that it has settled into your new homeostasis. You have moved beyond the period of pain or pleasure associated with alcohol. What drove you to stop has become a distant memory, so associations you originally had with alcohol are less powerful. In general, this is the ego inside of us that believes it has control, and since we are feeling so good, we don't think anything can change that – a typical thought process for someone when they break long-standing abstinence.

What we need to do in this case is set up long-term reminders to refer to in these situations – a useful tool to use during high stress or what we will see as breaking points. A mentor of mine shared a technique of planning and visualization that I have gone on to use successfully. I have added more visualization techniques here to anchor this into our minds. I will share this same technique here.

I need you to visualize two bottles on a shelf. The more detail you can create, the better. What does the room look like? What does the shelf look like? What color, shape, and size are the bottles? What does the cap or the cork look like? In my case, I make it one of those wine tops to open like a gross beer. Come up with an elaborate visualization.

Now I want you to take one bottle off the shelf – our pleasure bottle. We will fill this bottle with thoughts, emotions, and real-life examples of a life without alcohol. Fill this with all the pleasures you experience, such as more love, clarity, health, better relationships, and more money. Amazing sleep and confidence are other examples. Take it further and use an instance where your life is better without alcohol, like running a marathon or being up early to make your kids breakfast.

Think through a moment or a clip of a dream life scenario. Now, envision the life you dream of - the dream home, the loving relationship, wealth and prosperity, travel, and excitement. Give this real thought - the more detail, the better. Once it's filled, envision putting the top back on and placing it on the shelf.

Now take the other bottle off the shelf –our pain bottle. This time we will be filling it with the reasons that drove us to take the journey of pain - anxiety, tiredness, brain fog, irritability, poor health, poor relationships, and sleep. List them out. Now, think of an instance where alcohol has caused pain. Maybe you fight with your partner, maybe you sleep through an important obligation, or you can think of an experience that has created anxiety.

Finally, think of a life where alcohol has robbed you of your dream life. For example, aged and in poor health, divorced and estranged from family, working a low-standard career, or living an average life. These examples are extreme, but this is meant to be an extreme example. Fill the bottle to the brim, put the top back on, and visualize placing it on the shelf. Make it tailored to what you wouldn't want to happen if alcohol took control.

You have now created a powerful resource for you to use at any time. When you question why you are on this journey or when you begin to have thoughts of drinking again, here's how to use this:

- When you have these thoughts, see yourself in that room.
- See your hand reaching out, taking the pain bottle off the shelf, and opening it.

- Observe and feel all that is in that bottle - the consequences and the emotions, the pain you associate with a life held back by alcohol.
- Don't rush this; you may feel the urge to do so.
- Look at the bottle as a teacher that reminds you of important lessons about yourself.
- Close the bottle and place it back on the shelf.

Now comes the fun part. Reach back for the pleasure bottle and open it. Remind yourself of the true benefits and all the beauty of the life you dream of. Feel the emotions attached to all of that. Again, don't rush this. Take your time to soak it all in. Then visualize placing the cap back on and putting it on the shelf.

Take a moment to look at the bottles on the shelf. Attach your experience right now to each bottle. Maybe each bottle has its energy or color emanating from it. You must decide. Which bottle do you choose - pain or pleasure? When you contemplate bringing alcohol back into your life the way it was before, it is your decision. From this perspective, the answer seems simple. Of course, we would want to choose pleasure over pain. However, as I mentioned, our ego will do all it can to rationalize why we can drink. It will trick us into believing that there are no consequences to making such a decision. Perhaps it will be inconsequential for some, but for others, deciding to drink will only open and pour out the entire bottle of pain we created here.

Use this visualization technique whenever you have doubts. It's also a technique we can use as an affirmation, even in times of strength. Fill your bottles and open them for strength. It works.

Overview:

- After stopping alcohol consumption, a new normal can lead to forgetting the reasons for change.
- The ego may rationalize drinking again during high-stress or breaking points.
- Use the Visualization technique with two bottles: pleasure and pain
- Pleasure bottle: positive aspects of life without alcohol (e.g., better health, relationships, sleep)
- Pain bottle: negative consequences and emotions associated with alcohol consumption
- Use visualization techniques to remind oneself of the reasons for the journey and to make a conscious decision
- The technique can serve as an affirmation during times of strength or doubt

Life After

*"In the storybook of life, every decision turns a page,
leading us closer to the chapter where our dreams reside."*

- MIKE HARENBROOK.

The big question on your mind might be what happens after the 66-day program. It's okay if you don't have the answer even at the end. That's why it's time to self-evaluate, even if you haven't. You may realize you don't want to eliminate alcohol or discover that it's time to put the drink down for good. Alternatively, you might reduce the frequency and quantity of your drinking, leading to positive changes in your life. The ultimate goal is to shift your relationship with alcohol in a healthier direction. Let's explore some options for moving forward and how to approach them.

Reset: If you feel committed and don't want to return to drinking, consider committing to another 66 days. You've made it this far, proving it's something you can do. We know that the more distance you put between you and your drinking, the easier it becomes. Whether you've decided to quit for good or just for now, either approach works. Remember that 66 days is just an average – the actual range can be between 66 and 256 days. If you haven't reached the point where the new lifestyle feels natural, consider extending your commitment to solidify lasting changes.

Reintroduction: If, after 66 days, you're contemplating reintroducing alcohol, take some time for self-assessment. Reflect on how you dealt with urges and cravings during the program. Did they subside quickly, allowing you to go days or weeks without longing for a drink? Consider that habit formation can take anywhere from 66 to 256 days. It might be time to extend your commitment if you haven't reached the tipping point between old and new habits. Only when the change feels effortless should you decide whether or not to reintroduce alcohol.

Before making that final decision:
1. Ask yourself critical questions about your motivations, experiences, and goals:
2. Envision your dream life and consider whether alcohol has a place in it.
3. Evaluate the improvements you've experienced over the last 66 days, such as better health, sleep, and overall well-being.

Questions:
1. Did you achieve your goals by abstaining from alcohol during this period?
2. What negative effects has alcohol had on your life, health, and relationships in the past?
3. Have you experienced any negative consequences as a result of eliminating alcohol from your life, health, and relationships over the last 66 days?
4. What was the most challenging day or experience during this 66-day journey?
5. On your best day while drinking alcohol regularly, what did you accomplish or how did you handle difficult situations?
6. On your best day without alcohol, what did you accomplish or how did you handle difficult situations?
7. Overall, do you feel better or happier now compared to before?

Improvements in the last 66 days. Choose all that apply:

Health	Wellbeing	Productivity
Sleep	Anxiety	Clarity
Diet	Mood	Wake time
Overall health	Stress level	Energy level
Fitness stamina	Spirituality	Accomplishments

Proceed with Caution: Do so mindfully If you decide to return to drinking after a break. Several factors will determine the outcome, including the nature of your previous relationship with alcohol. If you can maintain a low-level, occasional drinking pattern without reverting to old habits, great. However, recognize that you're not alone if your drinking patterns escalate. Alcohol is an addictive substance, and managing consumption can be challenging.

Moving forward, approach alcohol consumption with intention and awareness. For those of you who are ready to reintroduce alcohol but want to do it consciously, I applaud your commitment to maintaining the positive changes you've made. Here are a few things to consider:

Set Boundaries: Establish clear limits on the frequency and quantity of your alcohol consumption. Maybe you only want to drink on weekends or limit yourself to one drink per social event. Whatever you decide, make sure these boundaries are clear and achievable.

Monitor Your Intake: Keep track of your alcohol consumption to ensure you're sticking to your boundaries. It can be as simple as making a mental note or using an app to log your drinks.

Engage in Mindful Drinking: When you decide to drink, take the time to savor it. Notice the flavors, aromas, and sensations associated with each sip. Being present and mindful will make you more likely to drink in moderation and appreciate the experience.

Stay Accountable: Share your intentions and boundaries with a trusted friend or family member. Having someone to support you and hold you accountable can be invaluable in maintaining your newfound balance with alcohol.

Reevaluate Regularly: Periodically reassess your relationship with alcohol and adjust your boundaries as needed. Remember, you're in control and can always choose to change your habits based on your personal growth and circumstances. Also, keep in mind some aspects that might make long-term moderation difficult:

- Genetics: A family history
- Environment
- Mental health
- Insufficient support systems
- Poor coping skills
- History of chronic or heavy alcohol use
- Early-life alcohol use
- Biological factors and brain chemistry
- Personal motivation and self-efficacy
- Traumatic experiences
- Relationship issues

If you have a few or several of these you identify with, it's essential to know you are at increased risk of returning to your original baseline.

I've gone through my trial-and-error journey, experimenting with different rules and scenarios for drinking. Ultimately, I discovered that 99.99% of the time, not drinking works best for me. In rare instances, I can have a few drinks without consequences, but even then, I often find that I don't enjoy alcohol as much as I used to. Your journey will be unique, and there's no one-size-fits-all solution. The only wrong path is returning to an unhealthy relationship with alcohol.

Overview:

- Post-66-day program: options for moving forward include reset, reintroduction, or cautious return to drinking.
- Reset: consider committing to another 66 days if the new lifestyle doesn't feel natural yet.
- Reintroduction: self-assess and envision a dream life before deciding to reintroduce alcohol.
- Proceed with Caution: set boundaries, monitor intake, engage in mindful drinking, stay accountable, and reevaluate regularly.
- Long-term moderation may be difficult due to genetics, environment, mental health, support systems, coping skills, alcohol use history, and personal motivation.
- Personal journeys differ; focus on maintaining a healthy relationship with alcohol.

Final Thoughts

My mission is to provide you with information and support that leads to significant, life-changing improvements. While I don't think alcohol is inherently bad, I see it for what it is—a beautifully packaged, mass-marketed poison. Remember, the definition of poison is a substance that can cause illness and death when consumed regularly, which is what alcohol does. Can we do a few unhealthy things like eat cake, smoke a cigar, or have an occasional beer without consequence? For some of us, yes. For some of us, that's impossible because of our previous habits. I want you to see this for yourself, change your habits, and live a better life without relying on alcohol to cope with stress or social events. A beautiful life lived with clarity, health, love, and well-being. I hope this book has helped you realize your potential and achieve all your dreams.

Embrace your journey with an open mind and heart, knowing that the path to a healthier relationship with alcohol is unique for each individual. By taking control of your habits, you can unlock a world of personal growth, improved well-being, and a more fulfilling life.

As you progress, remember to be kind to yourself, learn from your experiences, and celebrate your achievements. The road ahead may have challenges, but with determination, self-awareness, and the support of those around you, you can overcome any obstacle.

As we close this chapter and the book, I want to remind you that your journey doesn't end here. Taking control of your habits is an ongoing process, and you'll continue to learn and grow as you navigate the path ahead. Welcome it with enthusiasm and self-assurance, knowing that you can influence your future and achieve the life of your dream. Move forward with the belief that your potential knows no bounds.

"To exist is to change, to change is to mature, to mature is to go on creating oneself endlessly."

- HENRI BERGSON

Made in the USA
Coppell, TX
19 August 2024

36200624R00121